Swift for Absolute Beginners

Gary Bennett

Brad Lees

Apress®

Swift for Absolute Beginners

ISBN-13 (pbk): 978-1-4842-0887-8

ISBN-13 (electronic): 978-1-4842-0886-1

Managing Director: Welmoed Spahr
Lead Editor: Michelle Lowman
Development Editor: Douglas Pundick
Technical Reviewer: Stefan Kaczmarek
Editorial Board: Steve Anglin, Mark Beckner, Gary Cornell, Louise Corrigan, James DeWolf, Jonathan Gennick, Robert Hutchinson, Michelle Lowman, James Markham, Matthew Moodie, Jeff Olson, Jeffrey Pepper, Douglas Pundick, Ben Renow-Clarke, Gwenan Spearing, Matt Wade, Steve Weiss
Coordinating Editor: Kevin Walter
Copy Editor: Kim Wimpsett
Compositor: SPi Global
Indexer: SPi Global
Artist: SPi Global
Cover Designer: Anna Ishchenko

Distributed to the book trade worldwide by Springer Science+Business Media New York, 233 Spring Street, 6th Floor, New York, NY 10013. Phone 1-800-SPRINGER, fax (201) 348-4505, e-mail orders-ny@springer-sbm.com, or visit www.springeronline.com. Apress Media, LLC is a California LLC and the sole member (owner) is Springer Science + Business Media Finance Inc (SSBM Finance Inc). SSBM Finance Inc is a Delaware corporation.

For information on translations, please e-mail rights@apress.com, or visit www.apress.com.

Apress and friends of ED books may be purchased in bulk for academic, corporate, or promotional use. eBook versions and licenses are also available for most titles. For more information, reference our Special Bulk Sales–eBook Licensing web page at www.apress.com/bulk-sales.

Any source code or other supplementary material referenced by the author in this text is available to readers at www.apress.com or http://forum.xcelme.com. For detailed information about how to locate your book's source code, go to www.apress.com/source-code/.

Gary would like to dedicate this book to wife Stefanie and children, Michael, Danielle, Michelle, and Emily, for always supporing him.

Brad would like to dedicate this book to his wife Natalie for always supporting him. He couldn't do it without her.

Contents at a Glance

Contents

About the Authors

Gary Bennett is president of xcelMe.com, which provides iOS programming courses online. By day, Gary develops iOS apps professionally, and by night, he teaches iOS programming. For more than six years, Gary has taught thousands of students how to develop iPhone/iPad apps and has several popular apps in the iTunes App Store. Gary has a bachelor's degree in computer science and has worked for 25 years in the technology and defense industries. He served 10 years in the U.S. Navy as a nuclear engineer aboard two nuclear submarines. After leaving the Navy, Gary worked for several companies as a software developer, CIO, and president. As CIO, he helped take VistaCare public in 2002. Gary also coauthored two editions of *Objective-C for Absolute Beginners* and *iPhone Cool Projects* for Apress. He lives in Scottsdale, Arizona, with his wife Stefanie and their four children.

Brad Lees has more than 16 years of experience in application development and server management. He has specialized in creating and initiating software programs in financial institutions, credit card processing, point-of-sale systems, and real estate development.

His professional career highlights have been lead iOS developer at Apriva, owner of Innovativeware, product development manager for Smarsh, and vice president of application development for iNation. Brad also coauthored two editions of *Objective-C for Absolute Beginners*.

A graduate of Arizona State University, Brad and his wife Natalie reside in Phoenix with their five children.

About the Technical Reviewer

Stefan Kaczmarek has more than 15 years of software development experience specializing in mobile applications, large-scale software systems, project management, network protocols, encryption algorithms, and audio/video codecs. As chief software architect and cofounder of SKJM, LLC, Stefan developed a number of successful mobile applications including iCam (which has been featured on CNN, *Good Morning America*, and *The Today Show*, and which was chosen by Apple to be featured in the "Dog Lover" iPhone 3GS television commercial) and iSpy Cameras (which held the #1 Paid iPhone App ranking in a number of countries around the world including the United Kingdom, Ireland, Italy, Sweden, and South Korea). Stefan resides in Phoenix, Arizona, with his wife, Veronica, and their two children.

Acknowledgments

We would like to thank Apress for all their help in making this book possible. Specifically, we would like to thank Kevin Walter, our coordinating editor, and Michelle Lowman, our acquisitions editor, for helping us stay focused and overcoming many obstacles. Without Kevin and Michelle, this book would not have been possible.

Special thanks to Douglas Pundick, our development editor, for all his suggestions during the editorial review process to help make this a great book. Thanks to Kim Wimpsett, the copy editor, who made the book look great.

Introduction

Over the past three years, we've heard the following countless times:

- "I've never programmed before, but I have a great idea for an iPhone/iPad app."
- "Can I really learn to program the iPhone or iPad?"

To the latter we answer, "Yes, but you have to believe you can." Only you are going to tell yourself you can't do it.

For the Newbie

This book assumes you may have never programmed before. The book is also written for someone who may have programmed before but never using object-oriented programming (OOP) languages. There are several Swift books out there, but all of these books assume you have programmed before and know OOP and computer logic. We wanted to write a book that takes readers from knowing little or nothing about computer programming and logic to being able to program in Swift. After all, Swift is a native programming language for the iPhone, iPad, and Mac.

Over the past six years, we have taught thousands of students at xcelMe.com to be iPhone/iPad (iOS) developers. Many of our students have developed some of the most successful iOS apps in their category in the iTunes App Store. We have incorporated what we have learned in our first two courses, Introduction to Object-Oriented Programming and Logic and Swift for iPhone/iPad Developers, into this book.

For the More Experienced

Many developers who programmed years ago or programmed in a non-OOP language need a background in OOP and logic before they dive into Swift. This book is for you. We gently walk you through OOP and how it is used in iOS development to help make you a successful iOS developer.

How This Book Is Organized

You'll notice that we are all about successes in this book. We introduce the OOP and logic concepts in playgrounds and then move those concepts to Xcode and Swift. Many students are visual learners or learn by doing. We use both techniques. We'll walk you through topics and concepts with visual examples and then take you through step-by-step examples that reinforce the concepts.

We often repeat topics in different chapters to reinforce what you have learned and apply these skills in new ways. This enables new programmers to reapply development skills and feel a sense of accomplishment as they progress. Don't worry if you feel you haven't mastered a topic. Keep moving forward!

The Formula for Success

Learning to program is an interactive process between your program and you. Just like learning to play an instrument, you have to practice. You must work through the examples and exercises in this book. Understanding the concept doesn't mean you know how to apply it and use it.

You will learn a lot from this book. You will learn a lot from working through the exercises in this book. However, you will really learn when you debug your programs. Spending time walking through your code and trying to find out why it is not working the way you want is an unparalleled learning process. The downside of debugging is that a new developer can find it frustrating. If you have never wanted to throw your computer out the window, you will. You will question why you are doing this and whether you are smart enough to solve the problem. Programming is humbling, even for the most experienced developer.

Like a musician, the more you practice, the better you get. By practicing, we mean programming! You can do some amazing things as a programmer. The world is your oyster. Seeing your app in the iTunes App Store is one of the most satisfying accomplishments. However, there is a price, and that price is time spent coding and learning.

Having taught many students to become iOS developers, we have put together a formula for what makes students successful. Here is our formula for success:

- Believe you can do it. You'll be the only one who says you can't do this. So, don't tell yourself that.

- Work through all the examples and exercises in this book.

- Code, code, and keep coding. The more you code, the better you'll get.

- Be patient with yourself. If you were fortunate enough to have been a 4.0 student who could memorize material just by reading it, this will not happen with Swift coding. You are going to have to spend time coding.

- You learn by reading this book. You really learn by debugging your code.

- Use the free xcelMe.com webinars and YouTube videos explained at the end of this introduction. The free live and recorded training videos will be invaluable in quickly becoming a successful iOS developer.

- Don't give up!

The Development Technology Stack

We will walk you through the development process for your iOS apps and what technology you need. However, briefly looking at all the technology pieces together is helpful. These are the key iOS development technologies you will need to know in order to build a successful app and get it on the App Store:

- Apple's developer website
- iTunes Connect
- Xcode
- Swift
- Object-oriented programming and logic
- Debugging
- Performance tuning

We know this is a lot of technology. Don't worry, we will go through it, and you will become comfortable using it.

Required Software, Materials, and Equipment

One of the great things about developing iOS apps is that everything you need to develop your app is free.

- Xcode
- Swift
- OSX 10.10 Yosemite
- Integrated development environment
- iPhone and iPad simulators

All you need to get started is a Mac and knowledge of where to download everything. We will cover this.

Operating System and IDE

When developing iOS apps, you have to use Xcode and Mac OS X. You can download both of these for free from the Mac App Store.

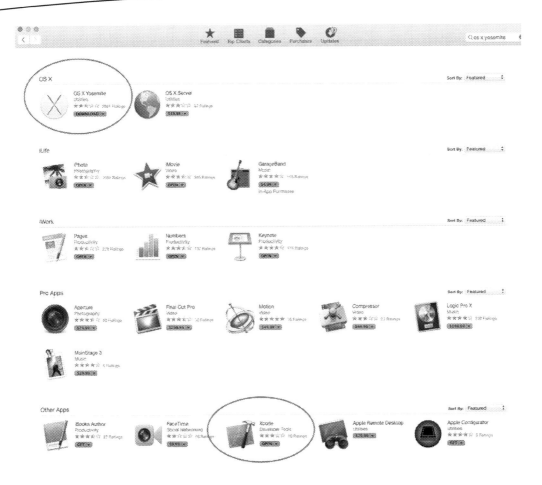

Software Development Kits

You will need to register as an iOS developer. You can do this for free at
`http://developer.apple.com/iphone`.

When you are ready to upload your app to the iTunes App Store, you will need to pay $99 per year in order to access.

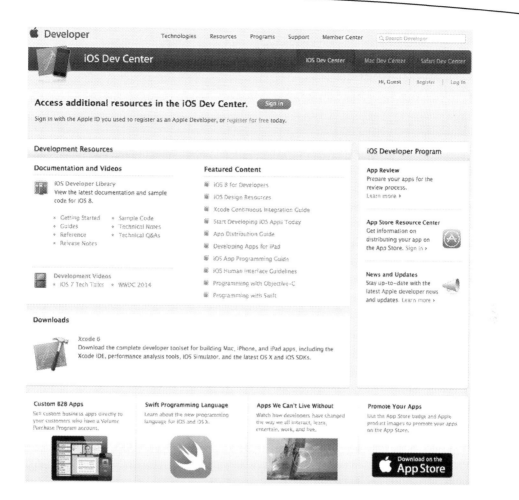

Dual Monitors

We recommend developers have a second monitor connected to their computers. It is great to step through your code and watch your output window and iOS simulator at the same time on dual independent monitors.

Apple hardware makes this easy. Just plug your second monitor into the display port of any Mac, with the correct Mini DisplayPort adapter, and you have two monitors working independently of one another. Note that dual monitors are not required. You will just have to organize your open windows to fit on your screen if you don't.

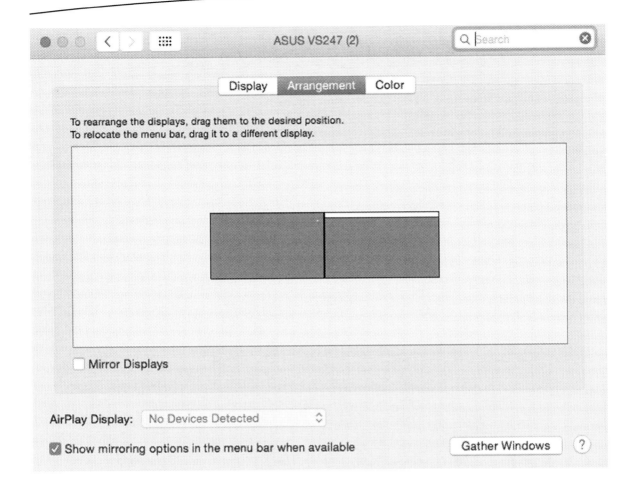

FREE LIVE WEBINARS, Q&A, AND YOUTUBE VIDEOS

Every Monday night at 5:30 p.m. Pacific time, we have live webinars and discuss a topic from the book or a timely item of interest. These webinars are free, and you can register for them at `www.xcelme.com/latest-videos/`.

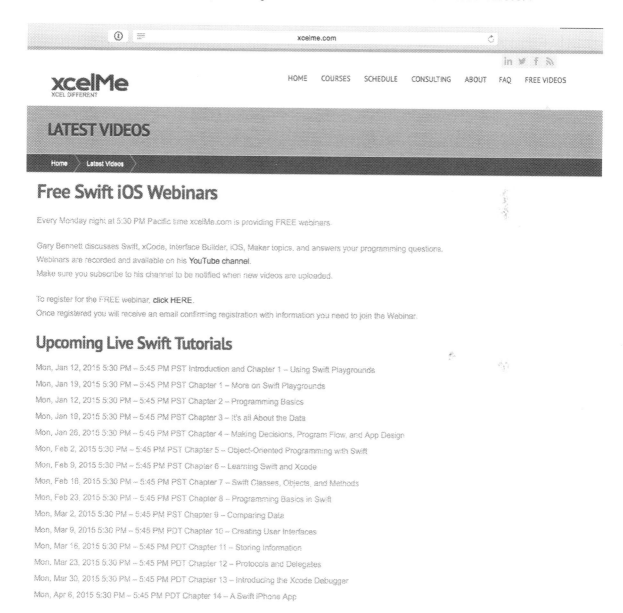

At the end of the webinars, we do a Q&A. You can ask a question on the topic discussed or on any topic in the book.

Additionally, all these webinars are recorded and available on YouTube. Make sure you subscribe to the YouTube channel so you are notified when new recordings are uploaded.

Free Book Forum

We have developed an online forum for this book at `http://forum.xcelme.com`, where you can ask questions while you are learning Swift and get answers from the authors. Also, Apple makes frequent changes to the programming language and SDK. We try our best to make sure any changes affecting the book get updated on the forum along with any significant text or code changes.

You can download the source code from the chapters on this forum too.

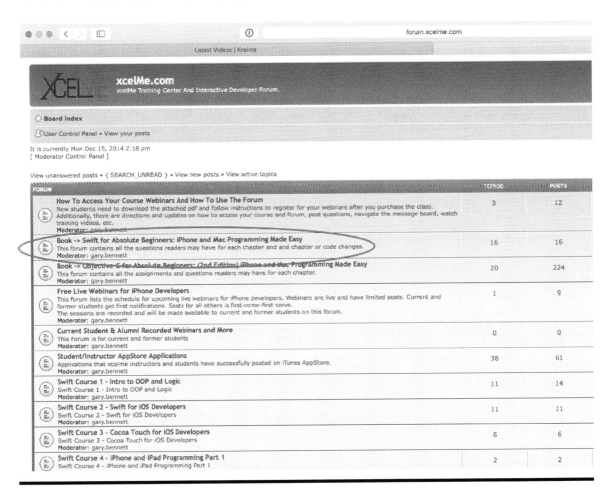

Becoming a Great iOS Developer

Now that you're ready to become a software developer and have read the introduction of this book, you need to become familiar with several key concepts. Your computer program will do exactly what you tell it to do—no more and no less. It will follow the programming rules that were defined by the operating system and the Swift programming language. Your program doesn't care if you are having a bad day or how many times you ask it to perform something. Often, what you think you've told your program to do and what it actually does are two different things.

> **Key to success** If you haven't already, take a few minutes to read the introduction of this book. The introduction shows you where to go to access the free webinars, forums, and YouTube videos that go with each chapter. Also, you'll better understand why this book uses the Swift playground programming environment and how to be successful in developing your iOS apps.

Depending on your background, working with something absolutely black and white may be frustrating. Many times, programming students have lamented, "That's not what I wanted it to do!" As you begin to gain experience and confidence in programming, you'll begin to think like a programmer. You will understand software design and logic, and you will experience having your programs perform exactly as you want and the satisfaction associated with this.

Thinking like a Developer

Software development involves writing a computer program and then having a computer execute that program. A *computer program* is the set of instructions that you want the computer to perform. Before beginning to write a computer program, it is helpful to list the steps that you want your program to perform in the order you want them accomplished. This step-by-step process is called an *algorithm*.

If you want to write a computer program to toast a piece of bread, you would first write an algorithm. This algorithm might look something like this:

1.   Take the bread out of the bag.

2.   Place the bread in the toaster.

3.   Press the toast button.

4.   Wait for the toast to pop up.

5.   Remove the toast from the toaster.

At first glance, this algorithm seems to solve the problem. However, the algorithm leaves out many details and makes many assumptions. Here are some examples:

■   What kind of toast does the user want? Does the user want white bread, wheat bread, or some other kind of bread?

■   How does the user want the bread toasted? Light or dark?

■   What does the user want on the bread after it is toasted: butter, margarine, honey, or strawberry jam?

■   Does this algorithm work for all users in their cultures and languages? Some cultures may have another word for toast or not know what toast is.

Now, you might be thinking this is getting too detailed for making a simple toast program. Over the years, software development has gained a reputation of taking too long, costing too much, and not being what the user wants. This reputation came to be because computer programmers often start writing their programs before they have really thought through their algorithms.

The key ingredients to making successful applications are *design requirements*. Design requirements can be formal and detailed or simple like a list on a piece of paper. Design requirements are important because they help the developer flush out what the application should do and not do when complete. Design requirements should not be completed in a programmer's vacuum but should be produced as the result of collaboration between developers, users, and customers.

Note   If you take anything away from this chapter, take away the importance of considering design requirements and user interface design before starting software development. This is the most effective (and least expensive) use of time in the software development cycle. Using a pencil and eraser is a lot easier and faster than making changes to code because you didn't have others look at the designs before starting to program.

Another key ingredient to your successful app is the *user interface* (UI) design. Apple recommends you spend more than 50 percent of the entire development process focusing on the UI design. The design can be done using simple pencil and paper or using Xcode's storyboard feature to lay out your screen elements. Many software developers start with the UI design, and after laying out all the screen elements and having many users look at paper mock-ups, they then write the design requirements from their screen layouts.

After you have done your best to flush out all the design requirements, laid out all the user interface screens, and had the clients or potential customers look at your design and give you feedback, coding can begin. Once coding begins, design requirements and user interface screens can change, but the changes are typically minor and easily accommodated by the development process. See Figures 1-1 and 1-2.

Figure 1-1. This is a UI mock-up of the account balance screen for an iPhone mobile banking app before development begins. This UI design mock-up was completed using OmniGraffle

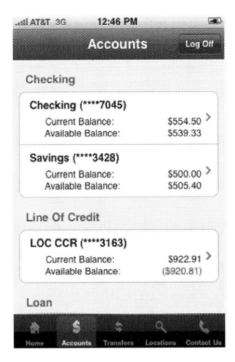

Figure 1-2. *This is a completed iPhone mobile banking application as it appeared on the iTunes App Store. This app is called Woodforest Mobile Banking*

Figure 1-1 shows a mock-up of a mobile banking app screen prior to development. Developing mock-up screens along with design requirements forces developers to think through many of the application's usability issues before coding begins. This enables the application development time to be shortened and makes for a better user experience and better reviews on the iTunes App Store. Figure 1-2 shows how the view for the mobile banking app appears when completed.

Completing the Development Cycle

Now that you have the design requirements and user interface designs and have written your program, what's next? After programming, you need to make sure your program matches the design requirements and user interface design and ensure that there are no errors. In programming vernacular, errors are called *bugs*. Bugs are undesired results of your programming and must be fixed before the app is released to the App Store. The process of finding bugs in programs and making sure the program meets the design requirements is called *testing*. Typically, someone who is experienced in software testing methodology and who didn't write the app performs this testing. Software testing is commonly referred to as *quality assurance* (QA).

> **Note** When an application is ready to be submitted to the iTunes App Store, Xcode gives the file an `.app` or `.ipa` extension, for example, `appName.app`. That is why iPhone, iPad, and Mac applications are called *apps*. This book will use *program*, *application*, and *app* to mean the same thing.

During the testing phase, the developer will need to work with QA staff to determine why the application is not working as designed. The process is called *debugging*. It requires the developer to step through the program to find out why the application is not working as designed. Figure 1-3 shows the complete software development cycle.

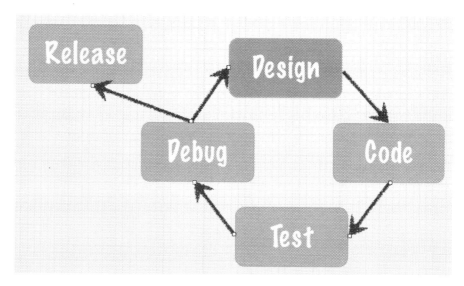

Figure 1-3. *The typical software development cycle*

Frequently during testing and debugging changes to the requirements (design) must occur to make the application more usable for the customer. After the design requirements and user interface changes are made, the process begins over again.

At some point, the application that everyone has been working so hard on must be shipped to the iTunes App Store. Many considerations are taken into account when this happens:

- Cost of development
- Budget
- Stability of the application
- Return on investment

There is always the give-and-take between developers and management. Developers want the app perfect, and management wants to start realizing revenue from the investment as soon as possible. If the release date were left up to the developers, the app would likely never ship to the App Store. Developers would continue to tweak the app forever, making it faster, more efficient, and more usable. At some point, however, the code needs to be pried from the developers' hands and uploaded to the App Store so it can do what it was meant to do.

Introducing Object-Oriented Programming

As discussed in detail in the introduction, playgrounds enable you to focus on *object-oriented programming* (OOP) without having to cover all the Swift programming syntax and complex Xcode development environment in one big step. Instead, you can focus on learning the basic principles of OOP and using those principles quickly to write your first programs.

For decades, developers have been trying to figure out a better way to develop code that is reusable, manageable, and easily maintained over the life of a project. OOP was designed to help achieve code reuse and maintainability while reducing the cost of software development.

OOP can be viewed as a collection of objects in a program. Actions are performed on these objects to accomplish the design requirements.

An *object* is anything that can be acted on. For example, an airplane, person, or screen/view on the iPad can all be objects. You may want to act on the plane by making the plane bank. You may want the person to walk or to change the color of the screen of an app on the iPad. Actions are all being applied to these objects; see Figure 1-4.

Figure 1-4. There are multiple objects in this view: cannons, balloons, and blimps. All objects can have actions applied—raise, lower, shoot, and so on

Playgrounds execute your code as you complete each line, such as the one shown in Figure 1-4. When you run your playground applications, the user can apply actions to the objects in your application. Xcode is an *integrated development environment* (IDE) that enables you to run your application from within your programming environment. You can test your applications on your computers first before running them on your iOS devices by running the apps in Xcode's simulator, as shown in Figure 1-5.

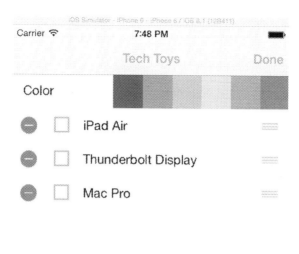

Figure 1-5. This sample iPhone app contains a table object to organize a list of tech toys. Actions such as "rotate left" or "user did select row 3" can be applied to this object

Actions that are performed on objects are called *methods*. Methods manipulate objects to accomplish what you want your app to do. For example, for a `jet` object you might have the following methods:

```
goUp
goDown
bankLeft
turnOnAfterBurners
lowerLandingGear
```

The table object in Figure 1-5 is actually called UITableView when you use it in a program, and it could have the following methods:

```
numberOfRowsInSection
cellForRowAtIndexPath
canEditRowAtIndexPath
commitEditingStyle
didSelectRowAtIndexPath
```

All objects have data that describes those objects. This data is defined as *properties.* Each property describes the associated object in a specific way. For example, the jet object's properties might be as follows:

```
altitude = 10,000 feet
heading = North
speed = 500 knots
pitch = 10 degrees
yaw = 20 degrees
latitude = 33.575776
longitude = -111.875766
```

For the UITableView object in Figure 1-5, the following might be the properties:

```
backGroundColor = Red
selectedRow = 3
animateView = No
```

An object's properties can be changed at any time when your program is running, when the user interacts with the app, or when the programmer designs the app to accomplish the design requirements. The values stored in the properties of an object at a specific time are collectively called the *state of an object.*

State is an important concept in computer programming. When teaching students about state, we ask them to go over to a window and find an airplane in the sky. We then ask them to snap their fingers and make up some of the values that the plane's properties might have at that specific time. Those values might be as follows:

```
altitude = 10,000 feet
latitude = 33.575776
longitude = -111.875766
```

Those values represent the state of the object at the specific time that they snapped their fingers.

After waiting a couple minutes, we ask the students to find that same plane, snap their fingers again, and record the plane's possible state at that specific point in time.

The values of the properties might then be something like the following:

```
altitude = 10,500 feet
latitude = 33.575665
longitude = -111.875777
```

Notice how the state of the object changes over time.

Working with the Playground Interface

Playgrounds offer a great approach in using the concepts just discussed without all the complexity of learning Xcode and the Swift language at the same time. It takes only a few minutes to familiarize yourself with the playground interface and begin writing a program.

Technically speaking, the playground interface is not a true IDE like you will be using to write your iOS apps, but it is pretty close and much easier to learn in. A true IDE combines code development, user interface layout, debugging tools, documentation, and simulator/console launching for a single application; see Figure 1-6. However, playgrounds offer a similar look, feel, and features to the Xcode IDE you develop apps with.

Figure 1-6. The Xcode IDE with the iPhone Simulator

In the next chapter, you will go through the playground interface and write your first program.

Summary

Congratulations, you have finished the first chapter of this book. It is important that you have an understanding of the following terms because they will be reinforced throughout this book:

- Computer program
- Algorithm
- Design requirements
- User interface
- Bug
- Quality assurance (QA)
- Debugging
- Object-oriented programming (OOP)
- Object
- Property
- Method
- State of an object
- Integrated development environment (IDE)

What's Next

The next 13 chapters provide the information you need to learn Swift and write iOS applications. Terms and concepts are introduced and reinforced over and over so you will begin to get more comfortable with them. Keep going and be patient with yourself.

Exercises

- Answer the following questions:
  - Why is it so important to spend time on your user requirements?
  - What is the difference between design requirements and an algorithm?
  - What is the difference between a method and a property?
  - What is a bug?
  - What is state?
- Write an algorithm for how a soda machine works from the time a coin is inserted until a soda is dispensed. Assume the price of a soda is 80 cents.
- Write the design requirements for an app that will run the soda machine.

Chapter 2

Programming Basics

This chapter focuses on the building blocks that are necessary to become a great Swift programmer. This chapter covers how to use the playground user interface, how to write your first Swift program, and how to use the Xcode integrated development environment (IDE).

> **Note** We will introduce you to using playgrounds, which will enable you to program right away without worrying about the complexities of Xcode. We have used this approach for the last five years and know that it helps you learn the concepts quickly, without discouragement, and gives you a great foundation to build upon.

Touring Xcode

Xcode and playgrounds make writing Swift code incredibly simple and fun. Type a line of code, and the result appears immediately. If your code runs over time, for instance through a loop, you can watch its progress in the timeline area. When you've perfected your code in the playground, simply move that code into your Swift iOS project. With Xcode, you can do the following:

- Design a new algorithm, watching its results every step of the way

- Create new tests, verifying that they work before promoting into your test suite

- Experiment with new APIs to hone your Swift coding skills

First you'll need to learn a little more about the Xcode user interface. When you open an Xcode iOS project, you are presented with a screen that looks like Figure 2-1.

Figure 2-1. Opening screen in Xcode with a Swift project

The Xcode user interface is set up to help you efficiently write your Swift applications. The user interface for playgrounds is similar to the user interface for an iOS application. You will now explore the major sections of Xcode's IDE workspace and playgrounds.

Exploring the Workspace Window

The workspace window, shown in Figure 2-2, enables you to open and close files, set your application preferences, develop and edit or app, and view text output and the error console.

Figure 2-2. Xcode's workspace window

The workspace window is your primary interface for creating and managing projects. The workspace window automatically adapts itself to the task at hand, and you can further configure the window to fit your work style. You can open as many workspace windows as you need.

The workspace window has four main areas: Editor, Navigator, Debug, and Utility.

When you select a project file, its contents appear in the Editor area, where Xcode opens the file in the appropriate editor.

You hide or show the other three areas by using buttons in the view selector in the toolbar.

Clicking this button shows or hides the Navigator area. This is where you view and maneuver through files and other facets of your project.

Clicking this button shows or hides the Debug area. This is where you control program execution and debug code.

Clicking this button shows or hides the Utilities area. You use the Utilities area for several purposes, most commonly to view and modify attributes of a file and to add ready-made resources to your project.

Navigating Your Workspace

You can access files, symbols, unit tests, diagnostics, and other facets of your project from the Navigator area. In the navigator selector bar, you choose the navigator suited to your task. The content area of each navigator gives you access to relevant portions of your project, and each navigator's filter bar allows you to restrict the content that is displayed.

Choose from these options in the navigator selector bar:

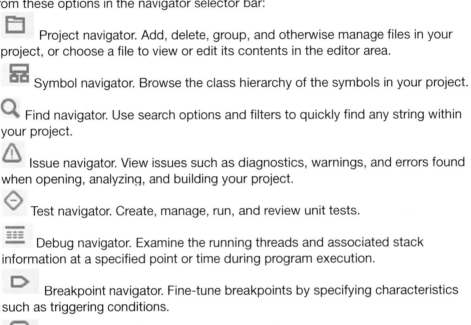 **Project navigator.** Add, delete, group, and otherwise manage files in your project, or choose a file to view or edit its contents in the editor area.

Symbol navigator. Browse the class hierarchy of the symbols in your project.

Find navigator. Use search options and filters to quickly find any string within your project.

Issue navigator. View issues such as diagnostics, warnings, and errors found when opening, analyzing, and building your project.

Test navigator. Create, manage, run, and review unit tests.

Debug navigator. Examine the running threads and associated stack information at a specified point or time during program execution.

Breakpoint navigator. Fine-tune breakpoints by specifying characteristics such as triggering conditions.

Report navigator. View the history of your builds, app console output, continuous integration, and source control tasks.

Editing Your Project Files

Most development work in Xcode occurs in the Editor area, which is the main area that is always visible within the workspace window. The editors you will use most often are as follows:

- *Source editor*: Write and edit Swift source code.
- *Interface Builder*: Graphically create and edit user interface files (see Figure 2-3).

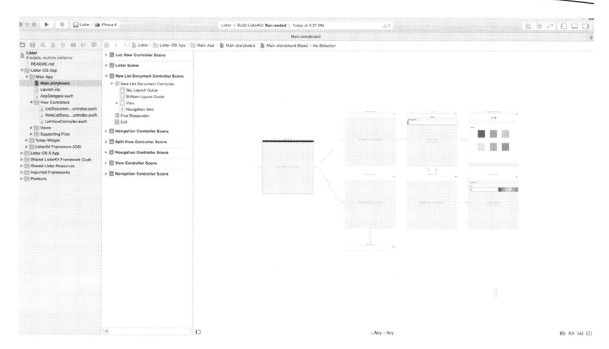

Figure 2-3. Xcode's Interface Builder

■ *Project editor*: View and edit how your apps should be built, such by specifying build options, target architectures, and app entitlements.

When you select a file, Xcode opens the file in an appropriate editor. In Figure 2-3, the file Main.storyboard is selected in the Project navigator, and the file is open in Interface Builder.

The editor offers three controls:

Clicking this button opens the Standard editor. You will see a single editor pane with the contents of the selected file.

Clicking this button opens the Assistant editor. You will see a separate editor pane with content logically related to that in the Standard editor pane.

Clicking this button opens the Version editor. You will see the differences between the selected file in one pane and another version of that same file in a second pane.

Creating Your First Swift Playground Program

Now that you have learned a little about Xcode, it's time to write your first Swift playground program and begin to understand the Swift language, Xcode, and some syntax. First you have to install Xcode.

Installing and Launching Xcode 6

Xcode 6 is available for download from the Mac App Store for free, as shown in Figure 2-4, and from the iOS Dev Center, as shown in Figure 2-5.

Figure 2-4. Xcode 6 is available for download from the Mac App Store for free

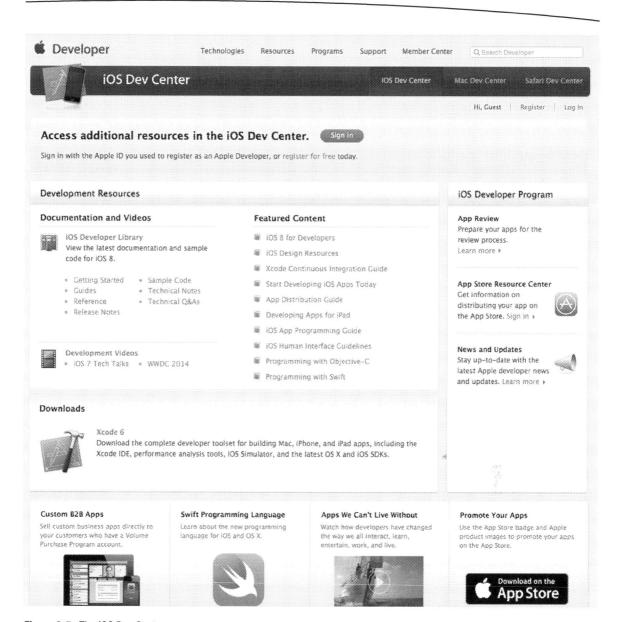

Figure 2-5. The iOS Dev Center

Note   This package has everything you need to write iOS apps. To develop iPhone apps, you will need to apply for the iPhone Developer Program and pay $99 (when ready to test on your iOS device and submit to the App Store). See `http://developer.apple.com`.

Now that you have installed Xcode, let's begin writing a Swift playground.

Launch Xcode and click "Get started with a playground," as shown in Figure 2-6.

Figure 2-6. Creating your first Swift playground

Using Xcode 6

After launching Xcode, follow these steps:

1. Let's name the playground **HelloWorld** and select iOS as the platform, as
    shown in Figure 2-7. Then click Next and save your app in the directory of
    your choice.

Figure 2-7. Name your playground HelloWorld and select iOS as the platform

Xcode does a lot of work for you and creates a playground file with code ready for you to use. It also opens your playground file in your Xcode editor so you can start, as shown in Figure 2-8.

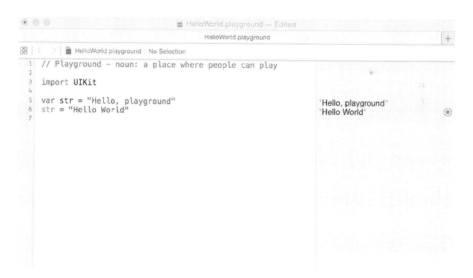

Figure 2-8. The playground app

You now need to become familiar with the Xcode IDE. Let's look at two of the most often used features.

- The Editor area
- The Results area

The Editor area is the business end of the Xcode IDE—where your dreams are turned into reality. It is where you write your code. As you write your code, you will notice it change color. Sometimes, Xcode will even try to autocomplete words for you. The colors have meanings that will become apparent as you use the IDE. The Editor area will also be the place where you debug your apps.

> **Note**   Even if I've mentioned it already, it is worth saying again: you will learn Swift programming by reading this book, but you will *really* learn Swift by debugging your apps. Debugging is where developers learn and become great developers.

Let's add a line of code to see the power of Swift playgrounds. Add line 6 shown in Figure 2-8. As soon as you enter the line of code, Xcode automatically executes the line and shows the result, "Hello World."

When you write Swift code, everything is important—commas, capitalization, and parentheses. The collection of rules that enable the compiler to compile your code to an executable app is called *syntax*.

Line 5 creates a string variable called str and assigns "Hello, playground" to the variable str.

Line 6 reassigns "Hello World" to the variable str.

Let's create a syntax error by entering line 8 shown in Figure 2-9.

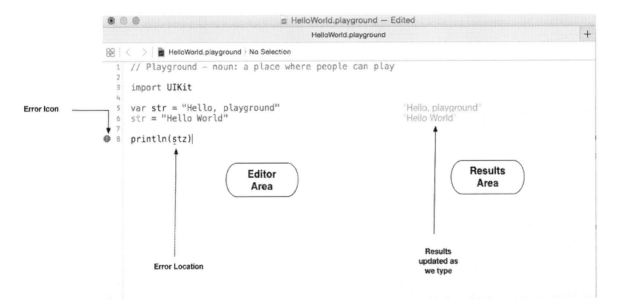

Figure 2-9. The playground with a syntax error caught by the Swift compiler

On line 8, `println` is a function that will print the contents of its parameters in the Results area. As you enter code, the Results area automatically updates with the results for each line of code that you entered.

Now, let's fix the app by spelling the `str` variable correctly, as shown in Figure 2-10.

Figure 2-10. Syntax error fixed

Feel free to play around and change the text that is printed. Have fun!

Summary

In this chapter, you built your first basic Swift playground app. I also covered new Xcode terms that are key to your understanding of Swift.

Key to Success   As mentioned in the introduction of the book, you can visit www.xcelme.com and click the Free Videos tab to view videos related to this chapter. The videos will help you understand more about Xcode, IDEs, and playgrounds. Also visit http://forum.xcelme.com to ask questions about these concepts.

The concepts that you should understand are as follows:

- Playground
- Editor area
- Results area
- Error icon

Exercise

- Extend your playground by adding a line of code that prints any text of your choosing.

Chapter **3**

It's All About the Data

As you probably know, data is stored as zeros and ones in your computer's memory. However, zeros and ones are not very useful to developers or app users, so you need to know how your program uses data and how to work with the data that is stored.

In this chapter, you will look at how data is stored on computers and how you can manipulate that data. You then use playgrounds to learn more about data storage.

Numbering Systems Used in Programming

Computers work with information differently than humans do. This section covers the various ways information is stored, tallied, and manipulated by devices such as your iPhone and iPad.

Bits

A *bit* is defined as the basic unit of information used by computers to store and manipulate data. A bit has a value of either 0 or 1. When computers were first introduced, transistors and microprocessors didn't exist. Data was manipulated and stored by vacuum tubes being turned on or off. If the vacuum tube was on, the value of the bit was 1, and if the vacuum tube was off, the value was 0. The amount of data a computer was able to store and manipulate was directly related to how many vacuum tubes the computer had.

The first recognized computer was called the Electronic Numerical Integrator and Computer (ENIAC). It took up more than 136 square meters and had 18,000 vacuum tubes. It was about as powerful as your handheld calculator.

Today, computers use transistors to store and manipulate data. The power of a computer processor depends on how many transistors are placed on its chip or central processing unit (CPU). Like the vacuum tube, transistors have an off or on state. When the transistor is off, its value is 0. If the transistor is on, its value is 1. Apple's A8 processor, which was introduced with the iPhone 6, has a dual-core ARM processor with more than 2 billion transistors (see Figure 3-1). This was up from 200 million transistors from the A5 processor and up from 149 million transistors on the A4 processor that was in iPhone 4 and the first iPad.

Figure 3-1. Apple's proprietary A8 processor (Source: Wikipedia)

Moore's Law

The number of transistors on your iPhone's or iPad's processor is directly related to your device's processing speed, graphics performance, memory capacity, and the sensors (accelerometer, gyroscope) available in the device. The more transistors, the more powerful your device is.

In 1965, the cofounder of Intel, Gordon E. Moore, described the trend of transistors in a processor. He observed that the number of transistors in a processor doubled every 18 months from 1958 to 1965 and would likely continue "for at least 18 months." The observation became famously known as Moore's law and has proven accurate for more than 55 years (see Figure 3-2).

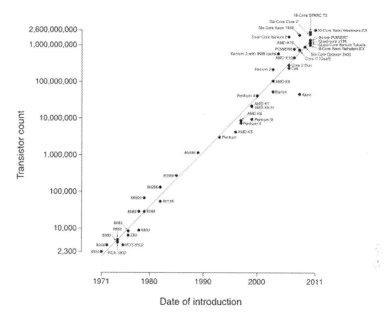

Figure 3-2. *Moore's law (Source: Wikipedia)*

> **Note** There is a downside to Moore's law, and you have probably felt it in your pocket book. The problem with rapidly increasing processing capability is that it renders technology obsolete quickly. So, when your iPhone's two-year cell phone contract is up, the new iPhones on the market will be twice as powerful as the iPhone you had when you signed up. How convenient for everyone!

Bytes

A byte is another unit used to describe information storage on computers. A *byte* is composed of 8 bits and is a convenient power of 2. Whereas a bit can represent up to two different values, a byte can represent up to 2^8, or 256, different values. A byte can contain values from 0 to 255.

> **Note** In Chapter 13, we discuss Base-2, Base-10, and Base-16 number systems in more detail. However, we will introduce these systems in this chapter so you can understand data types.

The binary number system represents the numerical symbols 0 and 1. To illustrate how the number 71 would be represented in binary, you can use a simple table of 8 bits (1 byte), with each bit represented as a power of 2. To convert the byte value 01000111 to decimal, simply add up the on bits, as shown in Table 3-1.

Table 3-1. The Number 71 Represented as a Byte (64 + 4 + 2 + 1)

Power to 2	2^7	2^6	2^5	2^4	2^3	2^2	2^1	2^0
Value for "on" bit	128	64	32	16	8	4	2	1
Actual bit	0	1	0	0	0	1	1	1

To represent the number 22 in binary, turn on the bits that add up to 22, or 00010110, as shown in Table 3-2.

Table 3-2. The Number 22 Represented as a Byte (16 + 4 + 2)

Power to 2	2^7	2^6	2^5	2^4	2^3	2^2	2^1	2^0
Value for "on" bit	128	64	32	16	8	4	2	1
Actual bit	0	0	0	1	0	1	1	0

To represent the number 255 in binary, turn on the bits that add up to 255, or 11111111, as shown in Table 3-3.

Table 3-3. The Number 255 Represented as a Byte (128 + 64 + 32 + 16 + 8 + 4 + 2 + 1)

Power to 2	2^7	2^6	2^5	2^4	2^3	2^2	2^1	2^0
Value for "on" bit	128	64	32	16	8	4	2	1
Actual bit	1	1	1	1	1	1	1	1

To represent the number 0 in binary, turn on the bits that add up to 0, or 00000000, as shown in Table 3-4.

Table 3-4. The Number 0 Represented as a Byte

Power to 2	2^7	2^6	2^5	2^4	2^3	2^2	2^1	2^0
Value for "on" bit	128	64	32	16	8	4	2	1
Actual bit	0	0	0	0	0	0	0	0

Hexadecimal

Often, it will be necessary to represent characters in another format that is recognized by computers, namely, a hexadecimal format. You will encounter hexadecimal numbers when you are debugging your apps. The *hexadecimal* system is a base-16 number system. It uses 16 distinct symbols: 0 to 9 to represent the values 0 to 9 and A to F to represent the values 10 to 15. For example, the hexadecimal number 2AF3 is equal in decimal to $(2 \times 16^3) + (10 \times 16^2) + (15 \times 16^1) + (3 \times 16^0)$, or 10,995. Figure 3-3 shows the ASCII table of characters. Because 1 byte can represent 256 characters, this works well for Western characters. For example, hexadecimal 20 represents a space. Hexadecimal 7D represents a right curly brace (}).

Dec	Hx	Oct	Char		Dec	Hx	Oct	Html	Chr	Dec	Hx	Oct	Html	Chr	Dec	Hx	Oct	Html	Chr
0	0	000	NUL	(null)	32	20	040	 	Space	64	40	100	@	@	96	60	140	`	`
1	1	001	SOH	(start of heading)	33	21	041	!	!	65	41	101	A	A	97	61	141	a	a
2	2	002	STX	(start of text)	34	22	042	"	"	66	42	102	B	B	98	62	142	b	b
3	3	003	ETX	(end of text)	35	23	043	#	#	67	43	103	C	C	99	63	143	c	c
4	4	004	EOT	(end of transmission)	36	24	044	$	$	68	44	104	D	D	100	64	144	d	d
5	5	005	ENQ	(enquiry)	37	25	045	%	%	69	45	105	E	E	101	65	145	e	e
6	6	006	ACK	(acknowledge)	38	26	046	&	&	70	46	106	F	F	102	66	146	f	f
7	7	007	BEL	(bell)	39	27	047	'	'	71	47	107	G	G	103	67	147	g	g
8	8	010	BS	(backspace)	40	28	050	(	(	72	48	110	H	H	104	68	150	h	h
9	9	011	TAB	(horizontal tab)	41	29	051	)	)	73	49	111	I	I	105	69	151	i	i
10	A	012	LF	(NL line feed, new line)	42	2A	052	*	*	74	4A	112	J	J	106	6A	152	j	j
11	B	013	VT	(vertical tab)	43	2B	053	+	+	75	4B	113	K	K	107	6B	153	k	k
12	C	014	FF	(NP form feed, new page)	44	2C	054	,	,	76	4C	114	L	L	108	6C	154	l	l
13	D	015	CR	(carriage return)	45	2D	055	-	-	77	4D	115	M	M	109	6D	155	m	m
14	E	016	SO	(shift out)	46	2E	056	.	.	78	4E	116	N	N	110	6E	156	n	n
15	F	017	SI	(shift in)	47	2F	057	/	/	79	4F	117	O	O	111	6F	157	o	o
16	10	020	DLE	(data link escape)	48	30	060	0	0	80	50	120	P	P	112	70	160	p	p
17	11	021	DC1	(device control 1)	49	31	061	1	1	81	51	121	Q	Q	113	71	161	q	q
18	12	022	DC2	(device control 2)	50	32	062	2	2	82	52	122	R	R	114	72	162	r	r
19	13	023	DC3	(device control 3)	51	33	063	3	3	83	53	123	S	S	115	73	163	s	s
20	14	024	DC4	(device control 4)	52	34	064	4	4	84	54	124	T	T	116	74	164	t	t
21	15	025	NAK	(negative acknowledge)	53	35	065	5	5	85	55	125	U	U	117	75	165	u	u
22	16	026	SYN	(synchronous idle)	54	36	066	6	6	86	56	126	V	V	118	76	166	v	v
23	17	027	ETB	(end of trans. block)	55	37	067	7	7	87	57	127	W	W	119	77	167	w	w
24	18	030	CAN	(cancel)	56	38	070	8	8	88	58	130	X	X	120	78	170	x	x
25	19	031	EM	(end of medium)	57	39	071	9	9	89	59	131	Y	Y	121	79	171	y	y
26	1A	032	SUB	(substitute)	58	3A	072	:	:	90	5A	132	Z	Z	122	7A	172	z	z
27	1B	033	ESC	(escape)	59	3B	073	;	;	91	5B	133	[	[	123	7B	173	{	{
28	1C	034	FS	(file separator)	60	3C	074	<	<	92	5C	134	\	\	124	7C	174	|		
29	1D	035	GS	(group separator)	61	3D	075	=	=	93	5D	135	]	]	125	7D	175	}	}
30	1E	036	RS	(record separator)	62	3E	076	>	>	94	5E	136	^	^	126	7E	176	~	~
31	1F	037	US	(unit separator)	63	3F	077	?	?	95	5F	137	_	_	127	7F	177	&#127;	DEL

Source: www.LookupTables.com

128	Ç	144	É	161	í	177	▓	193	┴	209	╤	225	ß	241	±
129	ü	145	æ	162	ó	178	▓	194	┬	210	╥	226	Γ	242	≥
130	é	146	Æ	163	ú	179	│	195	├	211	╙	227	π	243	≤
131	â	147	ô	164	ñ	180	┤	196	─	212	╘	228	Σ	244	⌠
132	ä	148	ö	165	Ñ	181	╡	197	┼	213	╒	229	σ	245	⌡
133	à	149	ò	166	ª	182	╢	198	╞	214	╓	230	µ	246	÷
134	å	150	û	167	º	183	╖	199	╟	215	╫	231	τ	247	≈
135	ç	151	ù	168	¿	184	╕	200	╚	216	╪	232	Φ	248	°
136	ê	152	ÿ	169	⌐	185	╣	201	╔	217	┘	233	Θ	249	∙
137	ë	153	Ö	170	¬	186	║	202	╩	218	┌	234	Ω	250	·
138	è	154	Ü	171	½	187	╗	203	╦	219	█	235	δ	251	√
139	ï	156	£	172	¼	188	╝	204	╠	220	▄	236	∞	252	ⁿ
140	î	157	¥	173	¡	189	╜	205	═	221	▌	237	φ	253	²
141	ì	158	₧	174	«	190	╛	206	╬	222	▐	238	ε	254	■
142	Ä	159	ƒ	175	»	191	┐	207	╧	223	▀	239	∩	255	
143	Å	160	á	176	░	192	└	208	╨	224	α	240	≡		

Source: www.LookupTables.com

Figure 3-3. ASCII characters

Unicode

Representing characters with a byte worked well for computers until about the 1990s, when the personal computer became widely adopted in non-Western countries where languages have more than 256 characters. Instead of a 1-byte character set, Unicode can have up to a 4-byte character set.

To facilitate faster adoption, the first 256 code points are identical to the ASCII character table. Unicode can have different character encodings. The most common encoding used for Western text is called UTF-8. As an iPhone developer, you will probably use this character encoding the most.

Data Types

Now that I've discussed how computers manipulate data, I will cover an important concept called *data types*. Humans can generally just look at data and the context in which it is being used to determine what type of data it is and how it will be used. Computers need to be told how to do this. So, the programmer needs to tell the computer the type of data it is being given. Here's an example: 2 + 2 = 4.

The computer needs to know you want to add two numbers together. In this example, they are integers. You might first believe that adding these numbers is obvious to even the most casual observer, let alone a sophisticated computer. However, it is common for users of iOS apps to store data as a series of characters, not a calculation. For example, a text message might read "Everyone knows that 2 + 2 = 4."

In this case, the example is a series of characters called a *string*. A data type is simply the declaration to your program that defines the data you want to store. A *variable* is used to store your data and is declared with an associated data type. All data is stored in a variable, and the variable has to have a variable type. For example, in Swift, the following are variable declarations with their associated data types:

```
var x = 10
var y = 2
var z = 0
var submarineName  = "USS Nevada SSBN-733"
```

Data types cannot be mixed with one another. You cannot do the following:

```
z = x + submarineName
```

Mixing data types will cause either compiler warnings or compiler errors, and your app will not run.

Swift is smart enough to know when you declare a variable what type it is: Int, Float, Double, String, Bool.

Table 3-5 gives examples of the basic data types in Swift.

Table 3-5. Swift Data Types

Type	Examples
Int	1, 5, 10, 100
Float or Double	1.0, 2.222, 3.14159
Bool	true, false
String	"Star Wars", "Star Trek"
ClassName	UIView, UiLabel, and so on

Declaring Constants and Variables

Swift constants and variables must be declared before they are used. You declare constants with the let keyword and variables with the var keyword. Constants never change during the program, but variables do change during the program.

There are two ways to declare variables: explicit and inferred.

Here is the syntax for explicit variables:

```
var name: type = value
var firstNumber: Int = 5
```

However, declaring the type is normally optional, and removing the type shortens the code and makes it easier.

Here is the syntax for inferred variables:

```
var name = value
var firstNumber = 5
```

You can use inferred most of the time because Swift is smart enough to figure out what the variable is by what you assign it.

If a variable isn't going to change, then you should declare it as a *constant*. Constants never change. Constants start with the keyword let, as shown here:

```
let secondNumber  = 10
```

To best understand how variables are declared, here are two examples:

```
let maximumNumberOfStudents = 30
var currentNumberOfStudents = 5
```

This code can be read as follows: "Declare a new constant called maximumNumberOfStudents, and give it a value of 30. Then, declare a new variable called currentNumberOfStudents, and give it an initial value of 5."

In this example, the maximum number of students is declared as a constant because the maximum value never changes. The current number of students counter is declared as a variable because this value must be incremented after the student enrollment change.

Most data you will use in your programs can be classified into three different types—Booleans, numbers, and objects. We will discuss how to work with numbers and object data types in the remainder of this chapter. In Chapter 4, we will talk more about Boolean data types when you learn how to write apps with decisionmaking.

> **Note**   Localizing your app is the process of writing your app so users can buy and use it in their native language. This process is too advanced for this book, but it is a simple one to complete when you plan from the beginning. Localizing your app greatly expands the total number of potential customers and revenue for your app without your having to rewrite it for each language. Be sure to localize your app. It is not hard to do and can easily double or triple the number of people who buy it. For more information on localizing your app, visit Apple's "Build Apps for the World" site: https://developer.apple.com/internationalization/

Optionals

Swift introduces an important concept called *optionals* that developers need to understand. Even for experienced iOS developers this concept is new. Optionals are not a hard topic to understand, but they take some time to get used to.

Use optionals when a value may be absent. An optional says the following:

- There is a value assigned to a variable *or* there is no value.

There are times when a constant or variable may or may not have a value. Listing 3-1 shows an example of the method toInt(), which converts a String value to an Int.

Listing 3-1. Converting a string to an integer

```
1 var myString = "42"
2 let someInteger = myString.toInt()
3 // someInteger is inferred to be of type "Int?", or "optional Int"
```

The constant someInteger is assigned the integer value 42. someInteger is also assigned the type of Int?. The question mark indicates that it is an optional type, meaning that the variable or constant's value may or may not be absent. See Listing 3-2.

Listing 3-2. Unable to convert a string to an integer

```
1 var myString = "Hello World"
2 let someInteger = myString.toInt()
3 // someInteger's value is now absent
```

Line 2 in Listing 3-2 has a problem. It is not possible to convert "Hello World" from a String to an Int. So, the value of someInteger is said to be absent or nil, because on line 2 someInteger is inferred to be an optional Int(Int?).

> **Note**   Objective-C programmers may have used nil to return an object from a method, with nil meaning "the absence of a valid object." This works for objects but not well for structures, basic C types, or enumeration values. Objective-C methods typically return a special value, like NSNotFound indicating the absence of a valid object. This assumes that the method's caller knows the special value to test against. Optionals indicate the absence of a value for *any type at all*, without using special constants.

The String's toInt() method might fail, so the method returns an *optional* Int, rather than an Int. An optional Int is written as Int?, not Int. Again, the question mark indicates that the value it contains is optional, meaning that it might contain *some* Int value, or it may contain *no value at all*. The value is either some Int or is nothing at all.

Swift's nil is not the same as nil in Objective-C. With Objective-C, nil is a pointer to a nonexistent object. In Swift, nil is not a pointer; it is the absence of a value. Optionals of any type can be set to nil, not just object types.

In Chapter 4 you will learn how to unwrap optionals and check for the object of a valid object.

Using Variables in Playgrounds

Now that you have learned about data types, let's write your code in a playground that adds two numbers and displays the sum.

1. Open Xcode, and select **Get started with a playground**, as shown in Figure 3-4.

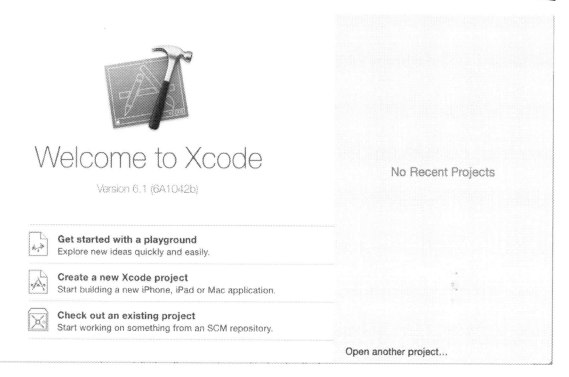

Figure 3-4. Creating a playground

2.   Name your playground **DataTypes**, as shown in Figure 3-5.

Figure 3-5. *Naming your playground*

3. When your playground is created, two lines of code are already placed in your code for you, as shown in Figure 3-6.

```
// Playground - noun: a place where people can play

import UIKit

var str = "Hello, playground"
```

Figure 3-6. *Two lines of code*

4. Enter the code of this playground, as shown in Listing 3-3.

Listing 3-3. Playground adding

```
1 // Playground - noun: a place where people can play
2
3 import UIKit
4
5 var str = "Hello, playground"
6
7 var firstNumber = 2
8 var secondNumber = 3
9
10 var totalSum = firstNumber + secondNumber
11
12 firstNumber = firstNumber + 1
13 secondNumber = secondNumber + 1
14
15 totalSum = firstNumber + secondNumber
16
17
18 println("totalSum = \(totalSum)")
```

Your playground should look like Figure 3-7.

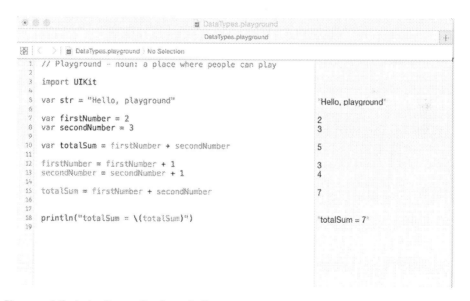

Figure 3-7. Playground displaying the results of your Swift app

One the neat features of playgrounds is that as you type in your code, Swift executes the line of code as you enter it so you can immediately view the results.

The // used in computer programming enables programmers to make comments about their code. Comments are not compiled by your applications and are used as notes for the programmer or, more importantly, for programmers who follow the original developer. Comments help both the original developer and later developers understand how the app was developed.

Sometimes, it is necessary for comments to span several lines or just part of a line. This can be accomplished with /* and */. All the text between /* and */ is treated as comments and is not compiled.

`println` is a function that can take one parameter and will print the contents of that parameter.

> **Note**   If your editor doesn't have the same menus or gutter (the left column that contains the line numbers of the program) you saw in the previous screenshots, you can turn these settings on in Xcode preferences. You can open Xcode preferences by clicking the Xcode menu in the menu bar and then selecting Preferences.

Summary

In this chapter, you learned about how data is used by your apps. You saw how to initialize variables and how to assign data to them. I explained that when variables are declared, they have a data type associated with them and that only data of the same type can be assigned to variables.

Exercises

- Write code within a Swift playground that multiplies two integers and displays the result.

- Write code within a Swift playground that squares a float. Display the resulting float.

- Write code within a Swift playground that subtracts two floats, with the result being stored as an integer. Note that rounding does not occur.

Chapter **4**

Making Decisions, Program Flow, and App Design

One of the great things about being an iOS developer is you get to tell your devices exactly what you want them to do and they do it—your devices will do tasks over and over again without getting tired. That's because iOS devices don't care how hard they worked yesterday, and they don't let feelings get in the way. These devices don't need hugs.

There is a downside to being a developer: you have to think of all the possible outcomes when it comes to your apps. Many students love having this kind of control. They enjoy focusing on the many details of their apps; however, it can be frustrating having to handle so many details. As I mentioned in the introduction to this book, there is a price to pay for developing apps, and that price is time. The more time you spend developing and debugging, the better you will get with all the details, and the better your apps will perform. You have to pay this price to become a successful developer.

Computers are black and white; there are no shades of gray. Your devices produce results, many of which are based on true and false conditions.

In this chapter, you will learn about computer logic and controlling the flow of your apps. Processing information and arriving at results are at the heart of all apps. Your apps need to process data based on values and conditions. To do this, you need to understand how computers perform logical operations and execute code based on the information your apps have acquired.

Boolean Logic

Boolean logic is a system for logical operations. Boolean logic uses binary operators such as AND and OR and the unary operator NOT to determine whether your conditions have been met. Binary operators take two operands. Unary operators take one operand.

I just introduced a couple of new terms that can sound confusing; however, you probably use Boolean logic every day. Let's look at a couple of examples of Boolean logic with the binary operators AND and OR in a conversation parents sometimes have with their teenage children:

"You can go to the movies tonight if your room is clean AND the dishes are put away."

"You can go to the movies tonight if your room is clean OR the dishes are put away."

Boolean operators' results are either TRUE or FALSE. In Chapter 3, I briefly introduced the Boolean data type. A variable that is defined as Boolean can contain only the values TRUE and FALSE.

```
var seeMovies: Bool = false
```

In the preceding example, the AND operator takes two operands: one to the left and one to the right of AND. Each operand can be evaluated independently with a TRUE or FALSE.

For an AND operation to yield a TRUE result, both sides of the AND have to be TRUE. In the first example, the teenager has to clean his or her room AND have the dishes done. If either one of the conditions is FALSE, the result is FALSE—no movies for the teenager.

For an OR operation to yield a TRUE result, only one operand has to be TRUE, or both conditions can be TRUE to yield a TRUE result. In the second example, just a clean bedroom would result in the ability to go to the movies.

> **Note**   In Objective-C and other programming languages, Boolean variables can hold integer variables; 0 represents FALSE, and any nonzero value represents TRUE. Swift's strong type checking doesn't allow this. Boolean variables in Swift can be assigned only `true` or `false`.

A NOT statement is a unary operator. It takes just one operand to yield a Boolean result. Here's an example:

"You can NOT go to the movies."

This example takes one operand. The NOT operator turns a TRUE operand to a FALSE and a FALSE operand to a TRUE. Here, the result is a FALSE.

> **Note**   A NOT operation turns a TRUE to a FALSE and a FALSE to a TRUE. Performing a NOT operation is commonly referred to as *flipping the bit* or *negating.*

AND, OR, and NOT are three common Boolean operators. Occasionally, you need to use more complex operators. XOR, NAND, and NOR are common operations for iOS developers.

The Boolean operator XOR means *exclusive-or*. An easy way to remember how the XOR operator works is the XOR operator will return a TRUE result if only one argument is TRUE, not both.

Swift does not have these operators built in, but consider that NAND and NOR mean NOT AND and NOT OR. After evaluating the AND or OR argument and the results, simply negate the results.

Truth Tables

You can use a tool to help you evaluate all the Boolean operators called a *truth table*, which is mathematical table used in logic to evaluate Boolean operators. They are helpful when trying to determine all the possibilities of a Boolean operator. Let's look at some common truth tables for AND, OR, NOT, XOR, NAND, and NOR.

In an AND truth table, there are four possible combinations of TRUE and FALSE.

- TRUE AND TRUE = TRUE

- TRUE AND FALSE = FALSE

- FALSE AND TRUE = FALSE

- FALSE AND FALSE = FALSE

Placing these combinations in a truth table results in Table 4-1.

Table 4-1. An AND Truth Table

A	B	A AND B
TRUE	TRUE	TRUE
TRUE	FALSE	FALSE
FALSE	TRUE	FALSE
FALSE	FALSE	FALSE

An AND truth table produces a TRUE result only if both of its operands are TRUE.

Table 4-2 illustrates an OR truth table and all possible operands.

Table 4-2. An OR Truth Table

A	B	A OR B
TRUE	TRUE	TRUE
TRUE	FALSE	TRUE
FALSE	TRUE	TRUE
FALSE	FALSE	FALSE

An OR truth table produces a TRUE result if one or both of its operands are TRUE.

Table 4-3 illustrates a NOT truth table and all possible operands.

Table 4-3. *A NOT Truth Table*

NOT	RESULT
TRUE	FALSE
FALSE	TRUE

A NOT *flips the bit* or negates the original operand's Boolean value.

Table 4-4 illustrates an XOR (or exclusive-or) truth table and all possible operands.

Table 4-4. *An XOR Truth Table*

A	B	A XOR B
TRUE	TRUE	FALSE
TRUE	FALSE	TRUE
FALSE	TRUE	TRUE
FALSE	FALSE	FALSE

The operator XOR yields a TRUE result if only one of the operands is TRUE.

Table 4-5 illustrates a NAND truth table and all possible operands.

Table 4-5. *A NAND Truth Table*

A	B	A NAND B
TRUE	TRUE	FALSE
TRUE	FALSE	TRUE
FALSE	TRUE	TRUE
FALSE	FALSE	TRUE

Table 4-6 illustrates a NOR truth table and all possible operands.

Table 4-6. A NOR Truth Table

A	B	A NOR B
TRUE	TRUE	FALSE
TRUE	FALSE	FALSE
FALSE	TRUE	FALSE
FALSE	FALSE	TRUE

The easiest way to look at the NAND and NOR operators is to simply negate the results from the AND and OR truth tables, respectively.

Comparison Operators

In software development, the comparison of different data items is accomplished with *comparison operators*. These operators produce a logical TRUE or FALSE result. Table 4-7 shows the list of comparison operators.

Table 4-7. Comparison Operators

>	Greater than
<	Less than
>=	Greater than or equal to
<=	Less than or equal to
==	Exactly equal to
!=	Not equal to

> **Note**   If you're constantly forgetting which way the greater-than and less-than signs go, use a crutch I learned in grade school: if the greater-than and less-than signs represent the mouth of an alligator, the alligator always eats the bigger value. It may sound silly, but it works.

Designing Apps

Now that I've introduced Boolean logic and comparison operators, you can start designing your apps. Sometimes it's important to express all or parts of your apps to others without having to write the actual code.

Writing code helps a developer think out loud and brainstorm with other developers regarding sections of code that are of concern—this helps to analyze problems and possible solutions before coding begins.

Pseudocode

Pseudocode refers to writing code that is a high-level description of an algorithm you are trying to solve. Pseudocode does not contain the necessary programming syntax for coding; however, it does express the algorithm that is necessary to solve the problem at hand.

Pseudocode can be written by hand on paper (or a whiteboard) or typed on a computer.

Using pseudocode, you can apply what you know about Boolean data types, truth tables, and comparison operators. Refer to Listing 4-1 for some pseudocode examples.

Listing 4-1. Pseudocode Examples Using Conditional Operators in if-then-else Code

```
int x = 5
int y = 6
isComplete  =  TRUE
if  x < y
{
    //in this example, x is less than 6
    do stuff
}
else
{
    do other stuff
}

if  isComplete == TRUE
{
    //in this example, isComplete is equal to TRUE
    do stuff
}
else
{
    do other stuff
}
//another way to check isComplete == TRUE
if isComplete
{
    //in this example,  isComplete is TRUE
    do stuff
}
```

```
//two ways to check if a value is false
if  isComplete == FALSE
{
     do stuff
}
else
{
     //in this example, isComplete is TRUE so the else block will be executed
          do other stuff
}
//another way to check isComplete == FALSE
if !isComplete
{
     do stuff
}
else
{
     //in this example,  isComplete is TRUE so the else block will be executed
          do other stuff
}
```

Note that ! switches the value of the Boolean it's applied to; so, using ! makes a TRUE value into a FALSE and makes a FALSE value into a TRUE.

Often, it is necessary to combine your comparison tests. A compound relationship test is one or more simple relationship tests joined by either && or || (two pipe characters).

&& and || are verbalized as logical AND and logical OR, respectively. The pseudocode in Listing 4-2 illustrates logical AND and logical OR operators.

Listing 4-2. Using && and || Logical Operators

```
int x = 5
int y = 6
isComplete  =  TRUE
//using the logical and
if x < y && isComplete == TRUE
{
    //in this example, x is less than 6 and isComplete == TRUE
    do stuff
}
if x < y || isComplete == FALSE
{
    //in this example, x is less than 6.
    //Only one operand has to be TRUE for an OR to result in a TRUE.
    //See Table 4-2 A OR Truth Table
    do stuff
}
```

```
//another way to test for TRUE
if x < y && isComplete
{
    //in this example, x is less than 6 and isComplete == TRUE
    do stuff
}
//another way to test for FALSE
if x < y && !isComplete
{
    do stuff
}
else
{
    // isComplete == TRUE
    do other stuff
}
```

Optionals and Forced Unwrapping

In Chapter 3 I introduced optionals. Optionals are variables that may or may not contain a value. Since optionals may not contain a value, you need to check for that before you access them.

You start by using an if statement to determine whether the optional contains a value by comparing the optional against nil. If the optional has a value, it is considered to be "not equal to" nil, as shown in Listing 4-3.

Line 4 in Listing 4-3 checks to see whether the optional variable is not equal to nil. In this example, the someInteger value is absent, and it is equal to nil, so line 8 code is executed.

Listing 4-3. Checking Whether an Optional Has a Value

```
1 var myString = "Hello world"
2 let someInteger = myString.toInt()
3 // someInteger's value is now absent
4 if someInteger != nil {
5     println("someInteger contains an integer value.")
6 }
7 else {
8     println("someInteger doesn't contain an integer value.")
9 }
```

Now that you have added a check to make sure your optional does or doesn't contain a value, you can access its value by adding an exclamation mark (!) to the end of the optional's name. The ! means you have checked to ensure the optional variable has a value and use it. This is called *forced unwrapping* of the optional's value. See Listing 4-4.

Listing 4-4. Forced Unwrapping

```
1 var myString = "42"
2 let someInteger = myString.toInt()
3 // someInteger contains a value
4 if someInteger != nil {
5     println("someInteger contains a value. Here it is: \(someInteger!)")
6 }
7 else {
8     println("someInteger doesn't contain an integer value.")
9 }
```

Optional Binding

You can find out whether an optional contains a value and, if so, assign a temporary constant or variable to that value in a single action. See Listing 4-5. This is called *optional binding*. Optional binding can be used with `if` and `while` statements to determine whether an optional has a value and, if so, extract the value to a constant or variable.

Listing 4-5. Optional Binding Syntax to a Constant

```
1 let someOptional: String? = "hello world"
2 if let constantName = someOptional {
3     println("constantName contains a value, Here it is: \(constantName)")
4 }
```

If you want to assign the optional to a variable so you can manipulate that variable, you can assign the optional to a var, as shown in Listing 4-6.

Listing 4-6. Optional Binding Syntax to a Variable

```
1 let someOptional: String? = "hello world"
2 if var variableName = someOptional {
3     println("variableName contains a value, Here it is: \(variableName)")
4     }
```

Notice in Listings 4-5 and 4-6 you didn't need to use the `!`. If the conversion was successful, the variable or constant was initialized with the value contained within the optional, so the `!` was not necessary.

Implicitly Unwrapped Optionals

There are instances after the value is first set when you know that an optional will always have a value. In these instances, it's useful to remove the need to check and unwrap an optional every time it needs to be accessed. These kinds of optionals are called *implicitly unwrapped optionals*.

Because of the program's structure, you know that the optional has a value, so you can give permission for the optional to be safely unwrapped whenever it needs to be accessed. The ! is not needed every time you use it; instead, you place an ! after the optional's type when you declare it. Listing 4-7 shows the comparison between an optional String and an implicitly unwrapped optional String.

Listing 4-7. Comparison of an Optional String, and an Implicitly Unwrapped Optional String

```
1 var optionalString: String? = "My optional string."
2 var forcedUnWrappedString: String = optionalString! //requires an !
3
4 var nextOptionalString: String! = "An implicitly unwrapped optional."
5 var implicitUnwrappedString: String = nextOptionalString //no need for an !
```

Note   The following will trigger runtime exceptions: trying to access implicitly unwrapped optionals when they don't contain a value and attempting to unwrap an optional that does not contain a value.

Flowcharting

After the design requirements are finalized, you can create pseudocode sections of your app to solve complex development issues. *Flowcharting* is a common method of diagramming an algorithm. An algorithm is represented as different types of boxes connected by lines and arrows. Developers often use flowcharting to express code visually, as shown in Figure 4-1.

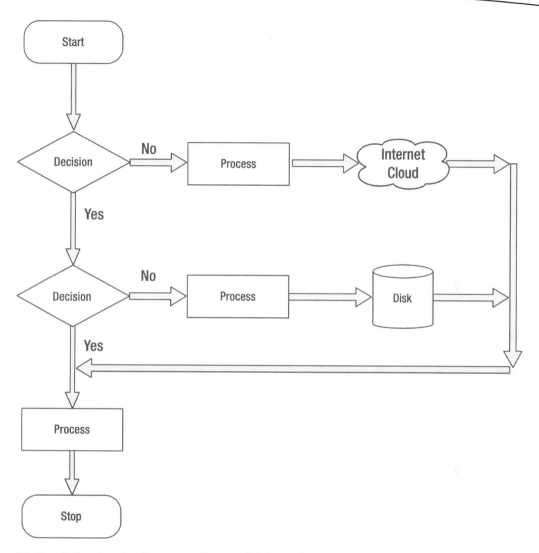

Figure 4-1. Sample flowchart showing common figures and their associated names

Flowcharts should always have a start and a stop. Branches should never come to an end without a stop. This helps developers make sure all of the branches in their code are accounted for and that they cleanly stop execution.

Designing and Flowcharting an Example App

I have covered a lot of information about decision making and program flow. It's time to do what programmers do best: write apps!

The app you have been assigned to write generates a random number between 0 and 100 and asks the user to guess the number. Users have to do this until the number is guessed. When users guess the correct answer, they will be asked if they want to play again.

The App's Design

Using your design requirements, you can make a flowchart for your app. See Figure 4-2.

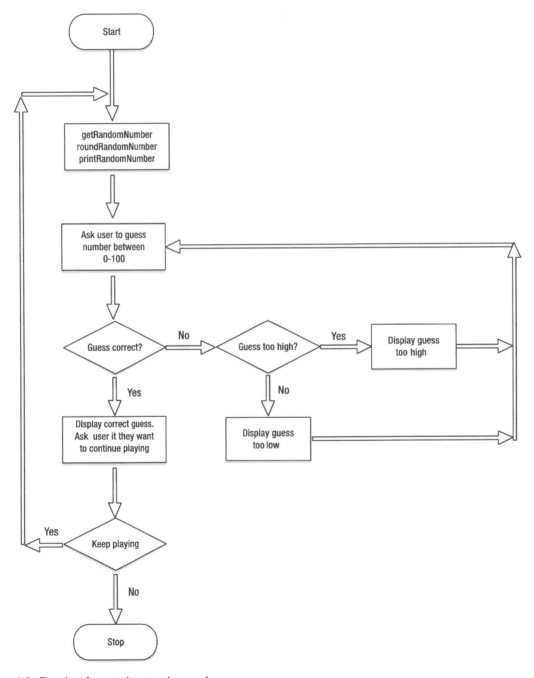

Figure 4-2. Flowchart for guessing a random number app

Reviewing Figure 4-2, you'll notice that as you approach the end of a block of logic in your flowchart, there are arrows that go back to a previous section and repeat that section until some condition is met. This is called *looping*. It enables you to repeat sections of programming logic—without having to rewrite those sections of code over—until a condition is met.

Using Loops to Repeat Program Statements

A *loop* is a sequence of program statements that is specified once but can be repeated several times in succession. A loop can repeat a specified number of times (count-controlled) or until some condition (condition-controlled) occurs.

In this section, you'll learn about count-controlled loops and condition-controlled loops. You will also learn how to control your loops with Boolean logic.

Count-Controlled Loops

A count-controlled loop is a loop that repeats a specified number of times. In Swift, this is a for loop. A for loop has a counter variable, which enables the developer to specify the number of times the loop will be executed. See Listing 4-8.

Listing 4-8. A Count-Controlled Loop

```
var i = 0

for i; i < 10; i++ {
    println("The index is: \(i)")
}
....continue
```

The loop in Listing 4-8 will loop ten times. The variable i starts at zero and increments at the end of the } by one. The incrementing is done by the i++ in the for statement; i++ is equivalent to i = i + 1. Then i is incremented by one to ten and checked to see whether it is less than ten. This for loop will exit when i = 10 and the } is reached.

> **Note**   It is common for developers to confuse the number of times they think their loops will repeat. If the loop started at 1 in Listing 4-8, the loop would repeat nine times instead of ten.

In Swift, for loops can have their counter variables declared in the for loop declaration. See Listing 4-9.

Listing 4-9. Counter Variable Initialized in the for Loop Declaration

```
for var i = 0; i < 10; i++ {
    println("The index is: \(i)")
}....continue
```

You use the `for-in` loop to iterate over collections of items, such as ranges of numbers, items in an array, or characters in a string.

Listing 4-10 prints a few entries in the ten times table.

Listing 4-10. Counter Variable Initialized in the for Loop Declaration

```
for index in 1...10 {
    println("\(index) times 10 is \(index * 10)")
}....continue
```

Condition-Controlled Loops

Swift has the ability to repeat a loop until some condition changes. You may want to repeat a section of your code until a false condition is reached with one of your variables. This type of loop is called a `while` loop. A `while` loop is a control flow statement that repeats based on a given Boolean condition. You can think of a `while` loop as a repeating `if` statement. See Listing 4-11.

Listing 4-11. A Swift while Loop Repeating

```
var isTrue = true
while isTrue
  {
    //do something
     isTrue = false // a condition occurs that sometimes sets isTrue to FALSE
  }
....continue
```

The `while` loop in Listing 4-11 first checks whether the variable `isTrue` is `true`—which it is—so the {loop body} is entered where the code is executed. Eventually, some condition is reached that causes `isTrue` to become `false`. After completing all the code in the loop body, the condition (`isTrue`) is checked once more, and the loop is repeated again. This process is repeated until the variable `isTrue` is set to `false`.

Infinite Loops

An infinite loop repeats endlessly, either because of the loop not having a condition that causes termination or because of the loop having a terminating condition that can never be met.

Generally, infinite loops can cause apps to become unresponsive. They are the result of a side effect of a bug in either the code or the logic.

Listing 4-12 is an example of an infinite loop caused by a terminating condition that can never be met. The variable x will be checked with each iteration through the while loop but will never be equal to 5. The variable x will always be an even number because it was initialized to zero and incremented by two in the loop. This will cause the loop to repeat endlessly. See Listing 4-13.

Listing 4-12. An Example of an Infinite Loop

```
var x = 0
while x != 5
 {
    //do something
    x = x + 2
 }
....continue
```

Listing 4-13. An Example of an Infinite Loop Caused by a Terminating Condition That Can Never Be Met

```
while true
{
    //do something forever
}
....continue
```

Coding the Example App in Swift

Using your requirements and what you learned, try writing your random number generator in Swift.

To program this app, you are going to have to leave the playground and do this as a Mac Console app. Unfortunately, at this time, a playground doesn't enable you to interact with a running app, so you are not able to capture keyboard input.

> **Note**   You can download the complete random number generator app at `http://forum.xcelme.com`. The code is in the Chapter 4 topic.

Your Swift app will run from the command line because it asks the user to guess a random number.

1. Open Xcode and start a new project. Choose the Command Line Tool project. See Figure 4-3.

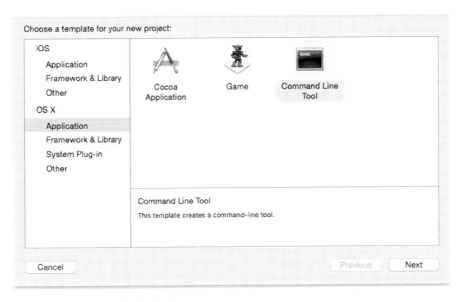

Figure 4-3. *Starting a new Command Line Tool project*

2. Call your project **RandomNumber** (see Figure 4-4). Select Language and make sure Swift is selected. Save the project anywhere you prefer on your hard drive.

Figure 4-4. *Project options for RandomNumber*

3. Open the main.swift file.

4. Write the code in Listing 4-14.

Listing 4-14. Source Code for Your Random Number Generator App

```
1 import Foundation
2
3 var randomNumber = 1
4 var userGuess = 1
5 var continueGuessing = true
6 var keepPlaying = true
7 var input = ""
8
9 while (keepPlaying) {
10     randomNumber = Int(arc4random_uniform(101)) //get a random number between 0-100
11     println("The random number to guess is: \(randomNumber)"  );
12     while (continueGuessing) {
13         println ("Pick a number between 0 and 100. ")
14         input = NSString(data: NSFileHandle.fileHandleWithStandardInput().
             availableData, encoding:NSUTF8StringEncoding)! //get keyboard input
15         input = input.stringByReplacingOccurrencesOfString("\n", withString: "",
             options: NSStringCompareOptions.LiteralSearch, range: nil) //strip off the /n
16         userGuess = input.toInt()!
17         if (userGuess == randomNumber) {
18             continueGuessing = false
19             println("Correct number!");
20         }
21             //nested if statement
22         else if (userGuess > randomNumber){
23             //user guessed too high
24             println("Your guess is too high");
25         }
26         else{
27             // no reason to check if userGuess < randomNumber. It has to be.
28             println("Your guess is too low");
29         }
30     }
31     println ("Play Again? Y or N");
32     input = NSString(data: NSFileHandle.fileHandleWithStandardInput().availableData,
         encoding:NSUTF8StringEncoding)!
33     input = input.stringByReplacingOccurrencesOfString("\n", withString: "", options:
         NSStringCompareOptions.LiteralSearch, range: nil)
34
35     if (input == "N" || input == "n"){
36         keepPlaying = false
37     }
38     continueGuessing = true
39 }
```

In Listing 4-14, there is new code that I haven't discussed before. The first new line of code (line 10) is as follows:

```
randomNumber = Int(arc4random_uniform(101))
```

This line will produce a random number between 0 and 100; arc4random_uniform() is a function that returns a random number.

The next line of new code is on line 14:

```
input = NSString(data: NSFileHandle.fileHandleWithStandardInput().availableData,
encoding:NSUTF8StringEncoding)!
```

This enables You to get keyboard input for the user. I will talk about this syntax in later chapters.

Nested if Statements and else-if Statements

Sometimes, it is necessary to nest if statements. This means that you need to have if statements nested inside an existing if statement. Additionally, it is sometimes necessary to have a comparison as the first step in the else section of the if statement. This is called an else-if statement (recall line 22 in Listing 4-14).

```
else if (userGuess > randomNumber)
```

Removing Extra Characters

Line 32 in Listing 4-14 is as follows:

```
input = input.stringByReplacingOccurrencesOfString("\n", withString: "", options:
NSStringCompareOptions.LiteralSearch, range: nil) //strip off the /n
```

Reading keyboard input can be difficult to work with. In this case, it leaves a remnant at the end of your string, \n, and you need to remove it. This is a *newline* character that is generated when the user presses the Return key on their keyboard.

Improving the Code Through Refactoring

Often, after you get your code to work, you examine the code and find more efficient ways to write it. The process of rewriting your code to make it more efficient, maintainable, and readable is called *code refactoring*.

As you review your code in Swift, you will often notice that you can eliminate some unnecessary code.

Design Requirements

As discussed in Chapter 1, the most expensive process in the software development life cycle is writing code. The least expensive process in the software development life cycle is gathering the requirements for your application; yet, this latter process is the most overlooked and least used in software development.

Design requirements usually begin by asking clients, customers, and/or stakeholders how the application should work and what problems it should solve.

With respect to apps, requirements can include long or short narrative descriptions, screen mock-ups, and formulas. It is far easier to open your word processor and change the requirements and screen mock-ups before coding begins than it is to modify an iOS app. The following is the design requirement for one view of an iPhone mobile banking app:

- *View*: Accounts view.

- *Description*: Displays the list of accounts the user has. The list of accounts will be in the following sections: Business Accounts, Personal Accounts and Car Loans, IRA, and Home Equity Loans.

- *Cells*: Each cell will contain the account name, the last four digits of the account, available balance, and present balance.

A picture is worth a thousand words. Screen mock-ups are helpful to developers and users because they can visualize how the views will look when they are completed. There are many tools that can quickly design mock-ups; one of these tools is OmniGraffle. See Figure 4-6 for an example of a screen mock-up used for design requirements generated by OmniGraffle.

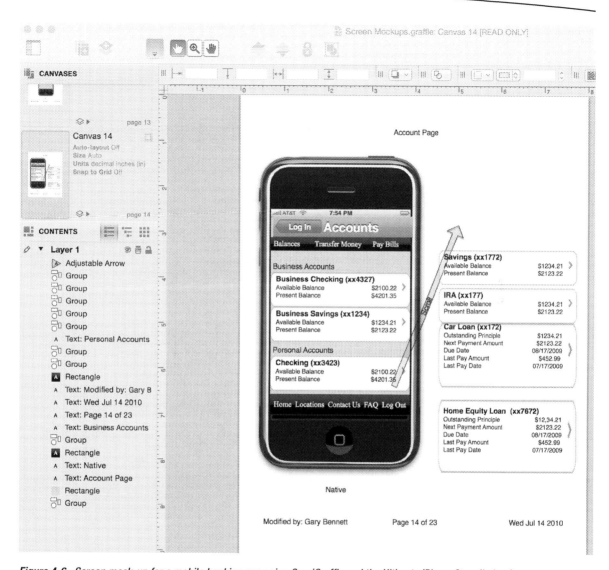

Figure 4-6. *Screen mock-up for a mobile banking app using OmniGraffle and the Ultimate iPhone Stencil plug-in*

Many developers believe that design requirements take too long and are unnecessary. There is a lot of information presented on the Accounts screen in Figure 4-6. Many business rules can determine how information is displayed to the user, along with all of the error handling when things go bad. When designing your app, working with all the business stakeholders at the beginning of the development process is critical to getting it right the first time.

Figure 4-7 is an example of all stakeholders being involved in your app's development. Having all stakeholders involved in every view from the beginning will eliminate multiple rewrites and application bugs.

Figure 4-7. Woodforest Mobile Banking app as it appears on the iTunes App Store; compare this with the app requirements Accounts screen in Figure 4-6

Additionally, Apple recommends that developers spend at least 50 percent of their development time on the user interface's design and development.

Balsamiq is also great tools for laying out your iOS app's look. See Figure 4-8.

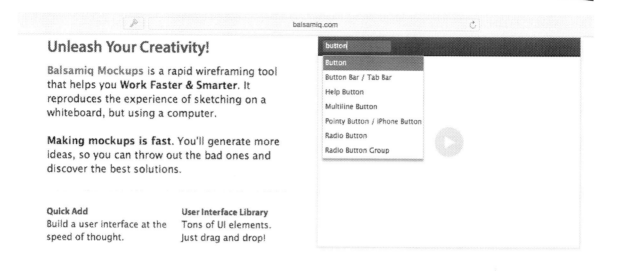

Unleash Your Creativity!

Balsamiq Mockups is a rapid wireframing tool that helps you **Work Faster & Smarter**. It reproduces the experience of sketching on a whiteboard, but using a computer.

Making mockups is fast. You'll generate more ideas, so you can throw out the bad ones and discover the best solutions.

Quick Add
Build a user interface at the speed of thought.

User Interface Library
Tons of UI elements. Just drag and drop!

Get Honest Feedback

Improve your designs by getting **immediate and meaningful feedback**. Sketch-style wireframes help focus the conversation on **content and interaction**, not minute details (those can come later).

Sketch-Style Controls
They look like sketches on purpose! It encourages brainstorming.

Clean Wireframes Option
Need to present your work? Switch to the clean wireframe skin!

Figure 4-8. Balsamiq.com web site for creating wireframe mock-ups

Summary

In this chapter, I've covered a lot of important information on how to control your applications; program flow and decision making are essential to every iOS app. Make sure you have completed the Swift example in this chapter. You might review these examples and think you understand everything without having to write this app. This will be a fatal mistake that will prevent you from becoming a successful iOS developer. You must spend time coding this example.

The terms in this chapter are important. You should be able to describe the following:

- AND
- OR
- XOR
- NAND
- NOR
- NOT
- Truth tables
- Negation
- All comparison operators
- Application requirement
- Logical AND (&&)
- Logical OR (||)
- Optionals and forced unwrapping
- Optional binding
- Implicitly unwrapped optionals
- Flowchart
- Loop
- Count-controlled loops
- For loop
- Condition-controlled loops
- Infinite loops
- while loops
- Nested if statements
- Code refactoring

Exercises

- Extend the random number generator app to print to the console how many times the user guessed before guessing the correct random number.
- Extend the random number generator app to print to the console how many times the user played the app. Print this value to the console when the user quits the app.

Object-Oriented Programming with Swift

Over the past 15 years, the programming world focused on the development paradigm of object-oriented programming (OOP). Most modern development environments and languages implement OOP. Put simply, OOP forms the basis of everything you develop today.

You may be asking yourself why we waited until Chapter 5 to present OOP using Swift if it is the primary development style of today. The simple answer is that it is not an easy concept for new developers. This chapter will go into detail about the different aspects of OOP and how this will affect your development.

Implementing OOP into your applications correctly will take some front-end planning, but you will save yourself a lot of time throughout the life of your projects. OOP has changed the way development is done. In this chapter, you will learn what OOP is. OOP was initially discussed in the first chapter of this book, but this chapter will go into more detail about it. You will revisit what objects are and how they relate to physical objects you find in the world. You will look into what classes are and how they relate to objects. You will also learn the steps you will need to take when planning your classes and some visual tools you can use to accomplish this. When you have read this chapter and have worked through the exercises, you will have a better understanding of what OOP is and why it is necessary for you as a developer.

At first, objects and object-oriented programming may seem difficult to understand, but the hope is that as you progress through this chapter, they will begin to make sense.

The Object

As discussed in Chapter 1, OOP is based on objects. Some of the discussion about objects will be a review, but it will also go into more depth. An object is anything that can be acted upon. To better understand what a programming object is, you will first look at some items in the physical world around you. A physical object can be anything around you that you can touch or feel. Take, for example, a television. Some characteristics of a television include type (plasma, LCD, or CRT), size (40 inches), brand (Sony, Vizio), weight, and cost. Televisions also have functions. They can be turned on or off. You can change the channel, adjust the volume, and change brightness.

Some of these characteristics and functions are unique to televisions, and some are not. For example, a couch in your house would probably not have the same characteristics as a television. You would want different information about a couch, such as material type, seating capability, and color. A couch might have only a few functions, such as converting to a bed or reclining.

Now let's talk specifically about objects as they relate to programming. An object is a specific item. It can describe something physical like a book, or it could be something such as a window for your application. Objects have properties and methods. Properties describe certain things about an object such as location, color, or name. Conversely, methods describe actions the object can perform such as close or recalculate. In this example, a TV object would have `type`, `size`, and `brand` properties, while a `Couch` object would have properties such as `color`, `material`, and `comfort level`. In programming terms, a property is a variable that is part of an object. For example, a TV would use a string variable to store the brand and an integer to store the height.

Objects also have commands the programmer can use to control them. The commands are called *methods*. Methods are the way that other objects interact with a certain object. For example, with the television, a method would be any of the buttons on the remote control. Each of those buttons represents a way you can interact with your television. Methods can and often are used to change the values of properties, but methods do not store any values themselves.

As described in Chapter 1, objects have a state, which is basically a snapshot of an object at any given point in time. A state would be the values of all the properties at a specific time.

In previous chapters, you saw the example of the bookstore. A bookstore contains many different objects. It contains book objects that have properties such as `title`, `author`, `page count`, and `publisher`. It also contains magazines with properties such as `title`, `issue`, `genre`, and `publisher`. A bookstore also has some nontangible objects such as a `sale`. A `sale` object would contain information about the books purchased, the customer, the amount paid, and the payment type. A `sale` object might also have some methods that calculate tax, print the receipt, or void the sale. A `sale` object does not represent a tangible object, but it is still an object and is necessary for creating an effective bookstore.

Because the object is the basis of OOP, it is important to understand objects and how to interact with them. You will spend the rest of the chapter learning about objects and some of their characteristics.

What Is a Class?

We cannot discuss OOP without discussing what a class is. A class defines which properties and methods an object will have. A class is basically a cookie cutter that can be used to create objects that have similar characteristics. All objects of a certain class will have the same properties and the same methods. The values of those properties will change from object to object.

A class is similar to a species in the animal world. A species is not an individual animal, but it does describe many similar characteristics of the animal. To understand classes more, let's look at an example of classes in nature. The Dog class has many properties that all dogs have in common. For example, a dog may have a name, an age, an owner, and a favorite activity. An object that is of a certain class is called an *instance* of that class. If you look at Figure 5-1, you can see the difference between the class and the actual objects that are instances of the class. For example, Lassie is an instance of the dog class. In Figure 5-1, you can see a Dog class that has four properties (Breed, Age, Owner, Favorite Activity). In real life, a dog will have many more properties, but these four are for this demonstration.

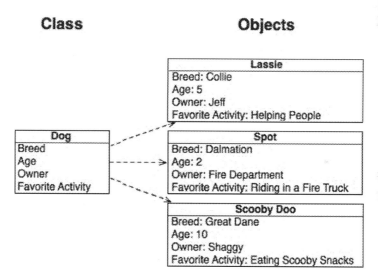

Figure 5-1. An example of a class and individual objects

Planning Classes

Planning your classes is one of the most important steps in your development process. While it is possible to go back and add properties and methods after the fact (and you will definitely need to do this), it is important that you know which classes are going to be used in your application and which basic properties and methods they will have. Spending time planning your different classes is important at the beginning of the process.

Planning Properties

Let's look at the bookstore example and some of the classes you need to create. First, it is important to create a `Bookstore` class. A `Bookstore` class contains the blueprint of the information each `Bookstore` object stores, such as the bookstore name, address, phone number, and logo (see Figure 5-2). Placing this information in a class rather than hard-coding it in your application will allow you to easily make changes to this information in the future. You will learn the reasons for using OOP methodologies later in this chapter. Also, if your bookstore becomes a huge success and you decide to open another one, you will be prepared because you can create another object of class `Bookstore`.

Bookstore
Name
Address1
Address2
City
State
Zip
Phone Number
Logo

Figure 5-2. The Bookstore class

Let's also plan a `Customer` class (see Figure 5-3). Notice how the name has been broken into `First Name` and `Last Name`. This is important to do. There will be times in your project when you may want to use only the first name of a customer, and it would be hard to separate the first name from the last if you didn't plan ahead. Let's say you want to send a letter to a customer letting them know about an upcoming sale. You do not want your greeting to say, "Dear John Doe." It would look much more personal to say, "Dear John."

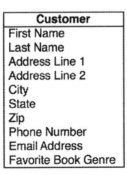

Customer
First Name
Last Name
Address Line 1
Address Line 2
City
State
Zip
Phone Number
Email Address
Favorite Book Genre

Figure 5-3. The Customer class

You will also notice how the address is broken into its different parts instead of grouping it all together. The `Address Line 1`, `Address Line 2`, `City`, `State`, and `ZIP` are separate. This is important and will be used in your application. Let's go back to the letter you want to send informing your customers of a sale in your store. You might not want to send it to all of the customers who live in different states. By separating the address, you can easily filter out those customers you do not want to include in your mailings.

We have also added the attribute of Favorite Book Genre to the Customer class. We added this to show you how you can keep many different types of information in each class. This field may come in handy if you have a new mystery title coming out and you want to send an e-mail alerting customers who are especially interested in mysteries. By storing this type of information, you will be able to specifically target different portions of your customer base.

A Book class is also necessary to create the bookstore (see Figure 5-4). You will store information about the book such as author, publisher, genre, page count, and edition number (in case there are multiple editions). The Book class will also have the price for the book.

Book
Author
Publisher
Genre
Year Published
Number of Pages
Edition
Price

Figure 5-4. The Book class

You can add another class called the Sale class (see Figure 5-5). This class is more abstract than the other classes discussed because it does not describe a tangible object. You will notice how we have added a reference to a customer and a book to the Sale class. Because the Sale class will track sales of books, you will need to know which book was sold and to which customer.

Sale
Customer
Book
Date
Time
Amount
Payment Type

Figure 5-5. The Sale class

Now that you know the properties of the classes, you need to look at some methods that each of the classes will have.

Planning Methods

You will not add all of the methods now, but the more planning you can do at the beginning, the easier it will be for you later. Not all of your classes will have many methods. Some may not have any methods at all.

> **Note**   When planning your methods, remember to have them focus on a specific task. The more specific the method, the more likely it is that it can be reused.

For the time being, you will not add any methods to the Book class or the Bookstore class. You will focus on your other two classes.

For the Customer class, you will add methods to list the purchase history of that client. There may be other methods that you will need to add in the future, but you will add just that one for now. Your completed Customer class diagram should look like Figure 5-6. The line near the bottom separates the properties from the methods.

Customer
First Name
Last Name
Address Line 1
Address Line 2
City
State
Zip
Phone Number
Email Address
Favorite Book Genre
List Purchase History

Figure 5-6. The completed Customer class

For the Sales class, we have added three methods. We added Charge Credit Card, Print Invoice, and Checkout (see Figure 5-7). For the time being, you do not need to know how to implement these methods, but you need to know that you are planning on adding them to your class.

Sale
Customer
Book
Date
Time
Amount
Payment Type
Charge Credit Card
Print Invoice
Checkout

Figure 5-7. The completed Sale class

Now that you have finished mapping out the classes and the methods you are going to add to them, you have the beginnings of a Unified Modeling Language (UML) diagram. Basically, this is a diagram used by developers to plan their classes, properties, and methods. Starting your development process by creating such a diagram will help you significantly in the long run. An in-depth discussion of UML diagrams is beyond the scope of this book. If you would like more information about this subject, smartdraw.com has a great in-depth overview of them; see www.smartdraw.com/resources/tutorials/uml-diagrams/.

Figure 5-8 shows the complete diagram.

Bookstore
Name
Address1
Address2
City
State
Zip
Phone Number
Logo

Sale
Customer
Book
Date
Time
Amount
Payment Type
Charge Credit Card
Print Invoice
Checkout

Book
Author
Publisher
Genre
Year Published
Number of Pages
Edition
Price

Customer
First Name
Last Name
Address Line 1
Address Line 2
City
State
Zip
Phone Number
Email Address
Favorite Book Genre
List Purchase History

Figure 5-8. *The completed UML diagram for the bookstore*

Implementing the Classes

Now that you understand the objects you are going to be creating, you need to create your first object. To do so, you will start with a new project.

1. Please launch Xcode. Click **File ➤ New ➤ Project**.

2. Select **iOS** on the left side. On the right side, select **Master-Detail Application**. For what you are doing in this chapter, you could have selected any of the application types (see Figure 5-9). Click Next.

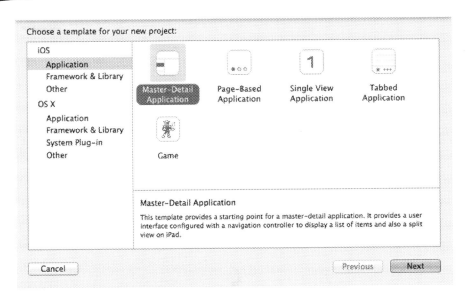

Figure 5-9. *Creating a new project*

3. You will have to enter a company name. Leave the check boxes on this screen as they appear by default. You will not be worrying about Core Data right now; it's discussed in Chapter 11. Also, leave the current Language selection to Swift. Select a location to save your project and then save your project. You can use the name BookStore or any other project name you want.

4. Select the **BookStore** folder from the Project navigator on the left side of the screen (see Figure 5-10). This is where the majority of your code will reside.

Figure 5-10. *Selecting the bookStore folder*

5. Select **File ➤ New ➤ File**.

6. From the pop-up window, select **Source** under the iOS header and then click **Swift File** on the right side (see Figure 5-11). Then click **Next**.

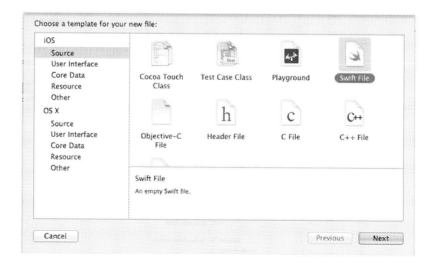

Figure 5-11. *Creating a new Swift file*

7. You will now be given the opportunity to name your file (see Figure 5-12). For this exercise, you will create the `Customer` class. For now, name the file `Customer`. Now click **Create**.

Figure 5-12. Creating the file

Note   For ease of use and for understanding your code, remember that class names should always be capitalized in Swift. Object names should always start lowercase. For example, Book would be an appropriate name for a class, and book would be a great name for an object based on the Book class. For a two-word object, such as the book author, an appropriate name would be bookAuthor. This type of capitalization is called *lower camel case*.

8. Now look in your main project folder; you should have a new file. It is called *Customer.swift*.

Note   If you had created a class in Objective-C, *Customer.h* and *Customer.m* files would have been created. The *.h* file is the header file that will contain information about your class. The header file will list all of the properties and methods in your class, but it will not actually contain the code related to them. The *.m* file is the implementation file, which is where you write the code for your methods.

9.   Click the *Customer.swift* file, and you will see the window shown in Figure 5-13. You will notice it does not contain a lot of information currently. The first part, with the double slashes (//), consists of comments and is not considered part of the code. Comments allow you to tell those who might read your code what each portion of code is meant to accomplish. All you have done this far in Swift is just create a file. You now need to add the code to the file to actually create a class. In your Swift file, type the following:

```
class Customer {

}
```

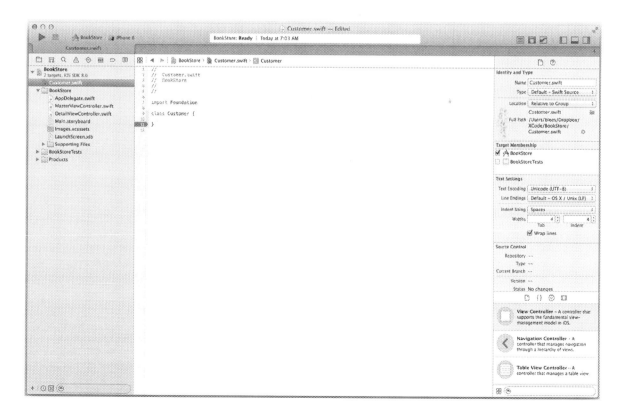

Figure 5-13. Your empty customer class

This is all that is needed to create a Customer class.

> **Note** In Swift, a class does not need to be in its own file. Many classes can be defined in a single Swift file, but this can be difficult to maintain when your project contains a lot of classes. It is usually cleaner to have a separate file for each class.

Now let's transfer the properties from the UML diagram to the actual class.

> **Tip** Properties should always start with a lowercase letter. There can be no spaces in a property name.

For the first property, First Name, add this line to your file:

```
var firstName = ""
```

This creates an object in your class called firstName. Notice you did not tell Swift what type of property firstName is. In Swift, you are able to declare a property, and that property will change its behavior based on the value we assign it. By giving the property an initial value of "", you tell the Swift compiler to make firstName a String.

> **Note** In Objective-C, all properties are required to declare a type. For example, to create the same firstName property, you would use the following code:
>
> ```
> NSString *firstName;
> ```
>
> This declares an NSString with the name firstName. In Swift, you declare only a variable and allow the system to determine the type.

Since all of the properties will be vars, you just need to repeat the same procedure for the other ones. When that is complete, your Swift file should look like Figure 5-14.

Figure 5-14. The Customer class interface with properties

Now that the class declaration is complete, you will need to add your method. Methods should be contained in the same class file and location as the properties. You will add a new method that returns an array. This code will look as follows:

```
func listPurchaseHistory() -> [String] {

        return ["Purchase 1","Purchase 2"]
}
```

This code might seem a little confusing. The empty parentheses tell the compiler that you are not passing any parameters to the method. The -> tells the system what you return from your method. [String] tells you that you are returning an array of strings. In the final version, you will actually want to return purchase objects, but you are using String for now. This code will not yet compile because you do not return an array, so you added a return of a simple array. That is all that needs to be done in the Swift file to create the class. Figure 5-15 shows the final Swift file.

Figure 5-15. The finished Customer class Swift file

Inheritance

Another major quality of OOP is inheritance. Inheritance in programming is similar to genetic inheritance. You might have inherited your eye color from your mother or hair color from your father, or vice versa. Classes can, in a similar way, inherit properties and methods from their parent classes, but unlike genetics, you do not inherit the values of those properties. In OOP, a parent class is called a *superclass*, and a child class is called a *subclass*.

> **Note**   In Swift, there is no superclass unless specifically stated.

You could, for example, create a class of printed materials and use subclasses for books, magazines, and newspapers. Printed materials can have many things in common, so you could define properties in the superclass of printed materials and not have to redundantly define them in each individual class. By doing this, you further reduce the amount of redundant code that is necessary for you to write and debug.

In Figure 5-16, you will see a layout for the properties of a `Printed Material` superclass and how that will affect the subclasses of `Book`, `Magazine`, and `Newspaper`. The properties of the `Printed Material` class will be inherited by the subclasses, so there is no need to define them explicitly in the class. You will notice that the `Book` class now has significantly fewer properties. By using a superclass, you will significantly reduce the amount of redundant code in your programs.

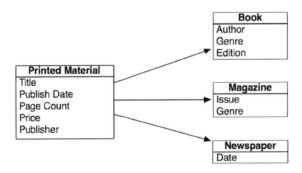

Figure 5-16. Properties of the super- and subclasses

Why Use OOP?

Throughout this chapter, I have discussed what OOP is and have even discussed how to create classes and objects. However, I think it is important to discuss why you want to use OOP principles in your development.

If you take a look at the popular programming languages of the day, all of them use the OOP principles to a certain extent. Swift, Objective-C, C++, Visual Basic, C#, and Java all require the programmer to understand classes and objects to successfully develop in those languages. In order to become a developer in today's world, you will need to understand OOP. But why use it?

It Is Everywhere

Just about any development you choose to do today will require you to understand object-oriented principles. On Mac OS X and in iOS, everything you interact with will be an object. For example, simple windows, buttons, and text boxes are all objects and have properties and methods. If you want to be successful as a programmer, you will need to understand OOP.

Eliminate Redundant Code

By using objects, you can reduce the amount of code you have to retype. If you write code to print a receipt when a customer checks out, you will want that same code available when you need to reprint a receipt. If you placed your code to print the receipt in the Sales class, you will not have to rewrite this code again. This not only saves you time but often helps you eliminate mistakes. If you do not use OOP and there is a change to the invoice (even something as simple as a graphic change), you have to make sure you make the change in your desktop application and the mobile application. If you miss one of them, you run the risk of having the two interfaces behave differently.

Ease of Debugging

By having all of the code relating to a book in one class, you know where to look when there is a problem with the book. This may not sound like such a big deal for a little application, but when your application gets to hundreds of thousands or even millions of lines of code, it will save you a lot of time.

Ease of Replacement

If you place all of your code in a class, then as things change in your application, you can change out classes and give your new class completely different functionality. However, it can interact with the rest of the application in the same way as your current class. This is similar to car parts. If you want to replace a muffler on a car, you do not need to get a new car. If you have code related to your invoice scattered all over the place, it makes it much more difficult to change items about a class.

Advanced Topics

I have discussed the basics of OOP throughout this chapter, but there are some other topics that are important to your understanding.

Interface

As I have discussed in this chapter, the way the other objects interact through each other is with methods. In Swift, you can set access levels on your methods. Declaring a method `Private` will make it accessible only to objects derived from it. By default, Swift methods are public and can be accessed by everyone. This is often called the *interface* because it tells other objects how they can interact with your objects. Implementing a standard interface throughout your application will allow your code to interact with different objects in similar ways. This will significantly reduce the amount of object-specific code you need to write.

Polymorphism

Polymorphism is the ability of an object of one class to appear and be used as an object of another class. This is usually done by creating methods and properties that are similar to those of another class. A great example of polymorphism that you have been using is the bookstore. In the bookstore, you have three similar classes: `Book`, `Magazine`, and `Newspaper`. If you wanted to have a big sale for your entire inventory, you could go through all of the books and mark them down. Then you could go through all of the magazines and mark them down and then go through all of the newspapers and mark them down. That would be more work than you would need to do. It would be better to make sure all of the classes have a markdown method. Then you could call that on all of the objects without needing to know which class they were as long as they were subclasses of a class that contained the methods needed. This would save a bunch of time and coding.

As you are planning your classes, look for similarities and methods that might apply to more than one type of class. This will save you time and speed up your application in the long run.

Summary

You've finally reached the end of the chapter! Here is a summary of the things that were covered:

- Object-oriented programming (OOP)
  - You learned about the importance of OOP and the reasons why all modern code should use this methodology.
- Object
  - You learned about objects and how they correspond to real-world objects. You learned that many programming objects relate directly to real-world objects. You also learned about abstract objects that do not correspond to real-world objects.
- Class
  - You learned that a class determines the types of data (properties) and the methods that each object will have. Every object needs to have a class. It is the blueprint for the object.

- Creating a class

  - You learned how to map out the properties and methods of your classes.

  - You used Xcode to create a class file.

  - You edited the Swift file to add your properties and methods.

Exercises

- Try creating the class files for the rest of the classes you mapped out.

- Map out an `Author` class. Choose the kind of information you would need to store about an author.

For the daring and advanced:

- Try creating a superclass called `PrintedMaterials`. Map out the properties that a class might have.

- Create classes for the other types of printed materials a store might carry.

Learning Swift and Xcode

For the most part, all computer languages perform the typical tasks any computer needs to do—store information, compare information, make decisions about that information, and perform some action based on those decisions. The Swift language makes these tasks easier to understand and accomplish. The real trick with Swift (actually, the trick with most programming languages) is to understand the symbols and keywords used to accomplish those tasks. This chapter continues the examination of Swift and Xcode so you can become even more familiar with them.

A Newcomer

As you may know, Swift has not been around for long. Development of the Swift language began about four years ago by Chris Lattner, and on September 9, 2014, Swift 1.0 was officially released. Swift borrows many ideas from Objective-C, but it also incorporates many features used by modern programming languages. Swift was designed from the ground up to be accessible to the average programmer.

Currently, there are two main types of programming languages. Compiled languages such as Objective-C and C++ are known for being rigid and requiring certain syntax. Compiled languages are also significantly faster in execution. Interpreted languages, such as Ruby, PHP, and Python, are known for being easier to learn and code but slower in their execution. Swift is a language to bridge the gap between the two. Swift incorporates the flexibility that makes interpreted languages so popular with the performance required for demanding applications and games. In fact, Apple claims Swift applications will perform faster than those written in Objective-C. In some of Apple's tests, Swift performed almost four times faster than Python and 40 percent faster than Objective-C.

Understanding the Language Symbols

Understanding symbols is a basic part of any programming language. Symbols are punctuation used to portray specific meanings in source code. Understanding the symbols of a language is required to be able to use the language. Here are some of the symbols and language constructs used in Swift, most of which you've already encountered in one way or another:

- {: This is the *begin* brace. It's used to start what's commonly referred to as a *block* of code. Blocks are used to define and surround a section of code and define its scope.

- }: This is the *end* brace. It's used to end a block of code. Wherever there is a begin ({), there must always be an accompanying end (}).

- []: These are the open and close brackets. They are used in the declaration and consumption of arrays.

- func methodName() -> String: This is how a Swift method is defined. The word methodName, of course, can represent any name. The word String can also change. It represents what type of information the method represents. In this example, String indicates the method will return a string, or a group of characters (data types were introduced in Chapter 3 and will be covered in more depth in later chapters). This will be discussed more later in the chapter.

- ;: The semicolon character is used to end a line of code. The thing to remember about a semicolon is that they aren't used at the end of statements that control the flow of the program, that is, if, for, while, and so on. You'll eventually understand the rules of where they go and don't go. In Swift, the semicolon is optional if you write only one instruction per line. For most of the examples in this book, you will omit the semicolon.

Figure 6-1 shows an example of Swift code.

```
Chapter6 > Chapter6 > ViewController.swift > No Selection
1     func logMessage() {
2         let hello = "Hello World!"
3         println(hello)
4     }
5
```

Figure 6-1. Example of Swift code

Line 1 represents a Swift function. The empty parentheses, (), indicates this function does not receive any variables. The fact that the parentheses are not followed by -> signifies that this function does not return any type of data and, if invoked, would not send a value to the caller.

The end of line 1 and line 4 are the braces that define a block of code. This block is what defines the method. Every method has at least one block.

Line 2 creates a constant name of `hello`. As you learned in previous chapters, a constant is a value that cannot change or is constant. The value of the constant `hello` is assigned "Hello World!" Because you assign `hello` to a `String` value, `hello` becomes a `String` and can use any method related to `Strings` (recall that you first saw strings in Chapter 3). Line 3 could be rewritten as follows:

```
let hello:String = "Hello World!"
```

Line 3 is a call to the `println` function. You pass the method the object to print the `hello` `String` object.

Although it does look a little cryptic to someone who is just learning Swift, the simple and terse syntax doesn't take too much time to learn.

Implementing Objects in Swift

Swift was built from the ground up to be object-oriented. It incorporates the best parts of Objective-C without the constraints of being compatible with C. It also takes some of the best features of a scripted language. The following are some of the concepts that make Swift object-oriented. Don't worry if some of these terms seem unfamiliar; they will be discussed in later chapters (Chapters 7 and 8 cover the basics).

- Pretty much everything is an *object.*
- Objects contain *instance* variables.
- Objects and instance variables have a defined *scope.*
- Classes hide an object's *implementation.*

> **Note**   As you saw in Chapter 5, the term *class* is used to represent, generically, the definition or type of an object. An *object* is what is created from the class. For example, an SUV is a *class* of vehicle. A class is a blueprint of sorts. A factory builds SUVs. The results are SUV objects that people drive. You can't drive a *class*, but you can drive an *object* built from a class.

So, how do these concepts translate to Swift? Swift is flexible in the implementation of classes.

> **Note**   Even though in Swift a single file may contain many different classes, a programmer will want to separate the code into different files to make access easier.

Let's look at a complete definition of a Swift class called `HelloWorld` (Figure 6-2).

```
 1 import Foundation
 2
 3
 4 class HelloWorld {
 5
 6     func logMessage() {
 7         let hello = "Hello World!"
 8         println(hello)
 9     }
10
11 }
```

Figure 6-2. HelloWorld class

In the preceding example, a class, `HelloWorld`, is being defined. This class has only one method defined: `logMessage`. What do all these strange symbols mean? Using the line numbers as a reference, you can review this code line by line.

Line 1 contains a compiler directive, `import Foundation`. For this little program to know about certain other objects, you need to have the compiler read other interface files. In this case, the Foundation file defines the objects and interfaces to the Foundation framework. This framework contains the definition of most non-user-interface base classes of the iOS and Mac OS X systems. You will not be using any Foundation framework–specific objects in this example, but it is a default part of any new Swift file.

The actual start of the object is on line 4, as follows:

```
class HelloWorld {
```

`HelloWorld` is the class. If you wanted `HelloWorld` to be a subclass of a logging class you had created, such as `LogFile`, you would change the declaration as follows:

```
class HelloWorld: LogFile {
```

Line 6 contains a method definition for this object, as follows:

```
func logMessage() {
```

When you're defining a method, you must decide whether you want the method to be a class or an instance method. In the case of the `HelloWorld` object, you are using the default method type, which is an instance. This method can be used *after* the object is created. If the words class are added before the func, the method can be used *before* the object is created. If you changed `logMessage` to a class method, it would be as follows:

```
class func logMessage() {
```

Lines 7 and 8 contain the body of the method. You learned about the details of the statements earlier in the chapter.

That's the complete description of class HelloWorld; there's not a whole lot here. More complicated objects simply have more methods and more variables.

But wait, there is more. Now that you have a new Swift class defined, how is it used? Figure 6-3 shows another piece of code that uses the newly created class.

```
let myHelloWorld = HelloWorld()
myHelloWorld.logMessage()
```

Figure 6-3. Calling a Swift method

The first line defines a constant called myHelloWorld. It then assigns the constant to an instance of the HelloWorld class. The second line simply calls the logMessage method of the myHelloWorld object. Those who have spent time in Objective-C will quickly see how much shorter and efficient both the class declaration and the object creation are in Swift.

> **Note**   Instantiation makes a class a real object in the computer's memory. A class by itself is not really usable until there is an instance of it. Using the SUV example, an SUV means nothing until a factory builds one (instantiates the class). Only then can the SUV be used.
>
> Method calls can also accept multiple arguments. Consider, for example, myCarObject. switchRadioBandTo(FM, 104.7). The method here would be switchRadioBandTo. The two arguments are contained in the parentheses. Being consistent in naming methods is critical.

Writing Another Program in Xcode

When you first open Xcode, you'll see the screen shown in Figure 6-4.

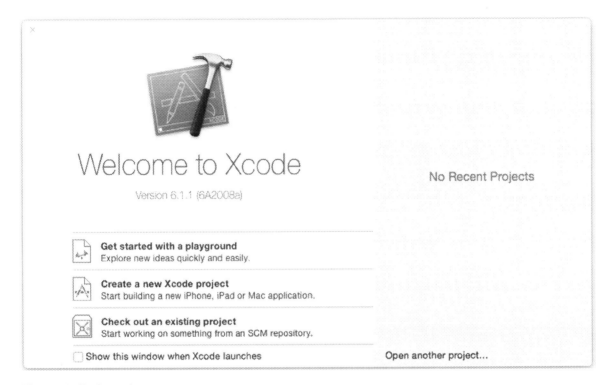

Figure 6-4. Xcode opening screen

You should always keep the screen in Figure 6-3 visible at the launch of Xcode. Until you are more comfortable with Xcode, keep the "Show this window when Xcode launches" check box selected. This window allows you to select the most recently created projects or create a new project from scratch.

Creating the Project

You are going to start a new project, so click the "Create a new Xcode project" icon. Whenever you want to start a new iOS or Mac OS X application, library, or anything else, use this icon. Once a project has been started and saved, the project will appear in the Recent list on the right of the display.

For this Xcode project, you will choose something simple. Make sure iOS Application is selected. Then select Single View Application, as shown in Figure 6-5. Then simply click the Next button.

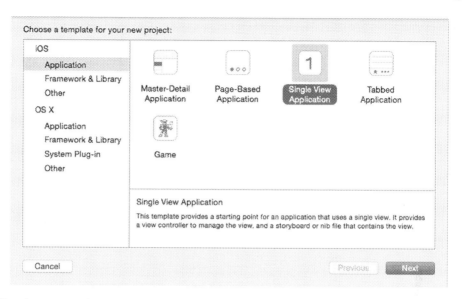

Figure 6-5. Choosing a new project from a list of templates

There are several types of templates. These templates make it easier to start a project from scratch in that they provide a starting point by automatically creating simple source files.

Once you've chosen the template and clicked the Next button, Xcode presents you with a dialog box asking for the project's name and some other information, as shown in Figure 6-6. Type a product name of **MyFirstApp**. The company Identifier needs to have some value, so enter **MyCompany**. Also make sure the Devices selection is set to iPhone.

Figure 6-6. Setting up the product name, company, and type

Once you've supplied all the information, click the Next button. Xcode will ask you where to save the project. You can save it anywhere, but the desktop is a good choice because it's always visible.

Once you've picked where to save the project, the main Xcode screen will appear (see Figure 6-7). In the leftmost pane is the list of source files. The right two-thirds of the screen is dedicated to the context-sensitive editor. Click a source file, and the editor will show the source code. Clicking a .storyboard file will show the screen interface editor.

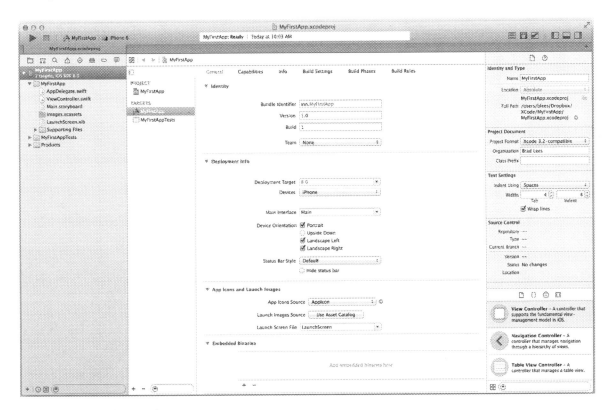

Figure 6-7. *The Xcode 6.1 main screen*

The first app is going to be simple. This iPhone app will contain a button. When the button is clicked, your name will appear on the screen. So, let's start by first looking more closely at some of the stub source code that Xcode built for you. The nice thing about Xcode is that it will create a stub application that will execute without any modification. Before you start adding some code, let's look at the main toolbar of Xcode, as shown in Figure 6-8.

Figure 6-8. *The Xcode 4 toolbar*

At first glance, there are three distinct areas of the toolbar. The left area is used to run and debug the application. The middle window displays status as a summary of compiler errors and warnings. The far-right area contains a series of buttons that customize the editing view.

As shown in Figure 6-9, the left portion of the toolbar contains a Play button that will compile and run the application. If the application is running, the Stop button will not be grayed out. Since it's grayed out, you know the application is not running. The scheme selection can be left alone for now. Schemas will be discussed in more detail in Chapter 13.

Figure 6-9. *Close-up of the left portion of the Xcode toolbar*

The right side of the Xcode toolbar contains buttons that change the editor. The three buttons represent the Standard editor (selected), the Assistant editor, and the Version editor. For now, just click the Standard Editor button, as shown in Figure 6-10.

Figure 6-10. *Close-up of the right portion of the Xcode toolbar*

Next to the editor choices are a set of View buttons. These buttons can be toggled on and off. For example, the one chosen in Figure 6-10 represents the current view shown in Figure 6-7, a list of the program files on the left third of the screen and the main editor on the remaining two-thirds. Any combination, or none, can be chosen to help customize the main workspace window. The last button opens the Utilities window. Chapter 13 discusses this button. For now, let's get back to your first iPhone app.

Click the ViewController.swift file, as shown in Figure 6-11. The editor shows some Swift code that defines a ViewController class.

Figure 6-11. *Looking at the source code in the Xcode editor*

You will notice two functions in the code. viewDidLoad is called immediately after a view is loaded and can be used for setting up the view. This is a good place to put code that sets up labels, buttons, colors, and so on. didReceiveMemoryWarning is called when your application is getting low on memory. You can use this function to decrease the amount of memory required by your application.

> **Note**   For now, you're simply going to add a few lines of code and see what they do. It's not expected that you understand what this code means right now. What's important is simply going through the motions to become more familiar with Xcode. Chapter 7 goes into more depth about what makes up a Swift program, and Chapter 10 goes into more depth about building an iPhone interface.

Next, you'll add a few lines of code into this file, as shown in Figure 6-12. Line 13 defines an iPhone label on the screen where you can put some text. Line 15 defines the method showName. You'll be calling this method in order to populate the iPhone label. A label is nothing more than an area on the screen where you can put some text information.

```
8
9    import UIKit
10
11   class ViewController: UIViewController {
12
13       @IBOutlet weak var nameLabel: UILabel!
14
15       @IBAction func showName(AnyObject) {
16           nameLabel.text = "My name is Brad!"
17       }
18
19       override func viewDidLoad() {
20           super.viewDidLoad()
21           // Do any additional setup after loading the view, typically from a nib.
22       }
23
24       override func didReceiveMemoryWarning() {
25           super.didReceiveMemoryWarning()
26           // Dispose of any resources that can be recreated.
27       }
28
29
30   }
31
32
```

Figure 6-12. Code added to the ViewController.h interface file

Caution   Type the code exactly as shown in the example. For instance, UILabel can't be uilabel or
UILABEL. Swift is a case-sensitive language, so UILabel is completely different from uilabel.

You will notice that the code you added has @IBOutlet and @IBAction in front of them. These
attributes are necessary when connecting objects with the interface designer. IBOutlet allows
you to control an interface object with code. IBAction allows you to execute code when something
happens in the interface such as tapping a button.

Note   IBOutlet and IBAction both start with IB, which is an acronym from Interface Builder. Interface
Builder was the tool used by NeXT and then Apple for building user interfaces.

You now have the necessary code in place, but you don't yet have an interface on the iPhone. Next,
you're going to edit the interface and add two interface objects to your app.

To edit the iPhone's interface, you need to click the Main.storyboard file once. The .storyboard file
contains all the information about a single window or view. Xcode 6 also supports .xib (pronounced
nib) files.

Note   Each .xib represents one screen on an iPhone or iPad. Apps that have multiple views will have
multiple .xib files, but many different views can be stored in each storyboard file.

You will use Xcode's interface editor to *connect* a UI object, such as a Label object, to the code you just created. Connecting is as easy as clicking and dragging.

Click the last view button in the upper-right part of the screen, as shown in Figure 6-13. This opens the Utilities view for the interface. Among other things, this Utilities view shows you the various interface objects you can use in your app. You're going to be concerned with only the first two: Button and Label. Figure 6-14 shows the Object Library. There are other libraries available, but for now you will be using only the third one from the left.

Figure 6-13. *The iPhone interface you're going to modify*

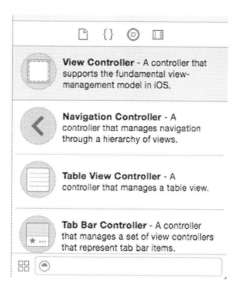

Figure 6-14. The Object Library

The first step is to click the button in the Utilities window. Next, drag the object to the iPhone view, as shown in Figure 6-15. Don't worry; dragging the object doesn't remove it from the list of objects in the Utilities view. Dragging it will create a new copy of that object on the iPhone interface.

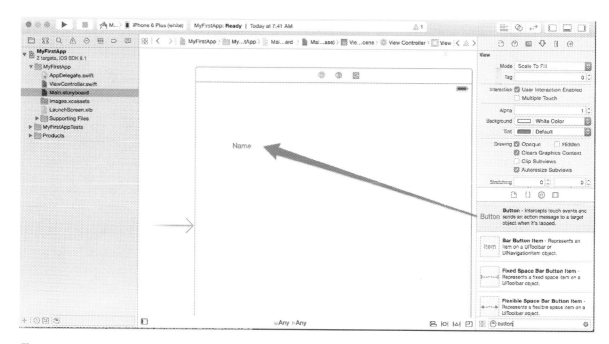

Figure 6-15. Moving a Button object onto the iPhone view

Next, double-click the Button that was just added to the iPhone interface. This allows the title of the Button to be changed from nothing to Name, as shown in Figure 6-16. Many different interface objects work just like this. Simply double-click, and the title of the object can be changed. This can also be done in the actual code, but it's much simpler to do it in Interface Builder.

Figure 6-16. *Modifying the Button object's title*

Once the title has been changed, drag a Label object to right below the Button, as shown in Figure 6-17.

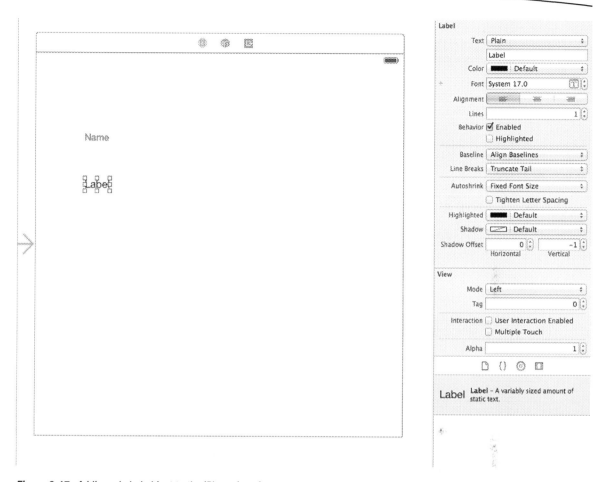

Figure 6-17. *Adding a Label object to the iPhone interface*

For now, you can leave the Label's text as "Label" since this makes it easy to find on the interface. If you clear the Label's text, the object will still be there, but there is nothing visible to click in order to select it. Expand the size of the Label by dragging the center white square to the right, as shown in Figure 6-18.

Figure 6-18. *Expanding the Label's size*

Now that you have both the Button and the Label, you can connect these visual objects to your program. Start by right-clicking (or Control-clicking) the Button control. This brings up a connection menu, as shown in Figure 6-19.

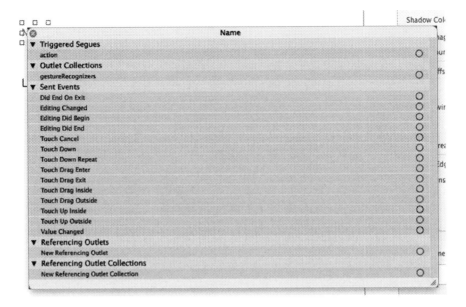

Figure 6-19. Connection menu for the Button object

Next, click and drag from the Touch Up Inside connection circle to the File's Owner icon, as shown in Figure 6-20. Touch Up Inside means the user clicked the *inside* the Button object. Dragging the connection to the View Controller connects the Touch Up Inside event to the `ViewController` object. This causes the object to be notified whenever the Button object is clicked.

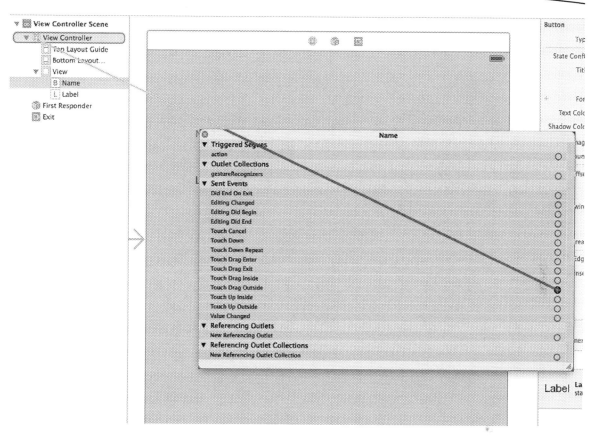

Figure 6-20. Connecting the Touch Up Inside event to the object

Once the connection is dropped, a list of methods that can be used in your connection is displayed, as shown in Figure 6-21. In this example, there is only one method, and that is the showName: method. Selecting the showName: method connects the Touch Up Inside event to the object.

Figure 6-21. Selecting the method to handle the Touch Up Inside event

Once the connection has been made, the details are shown on the Button's connection menu, as shown in Figure 6-22.

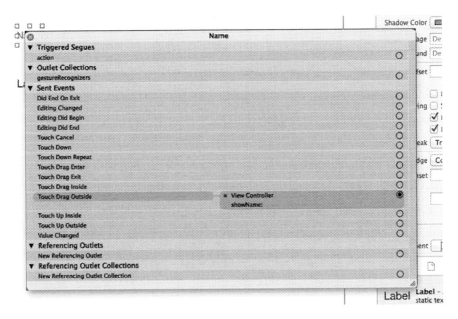

Figure 6-22. The connection is now complete

Next, you create a connection for the Label object. In this case, you don't care about the Label events; instead, you want to connect the ViewController's nameLabel outlet to the object on the iPhone interface. This connection basically tells the object that the Label you want to set text on is on the iPhone interface.

Start by right-clicking the Label object on the iPhone interface. This brings up the connection menu for the Label object, as shown in Figure 6-23. There are not as many options for a Label object as there were for the Button object.

Figure 6-23. Connection menu for the Label object

As mentioned, you are not here to connect an event. Instead, you connect what's referred to as a *referencing outlet*. This connection connects a screen object to a variable in your ViewController object. Just like the Button, drag the connection to the File's Owner icon, as shown in Figure 6-24.

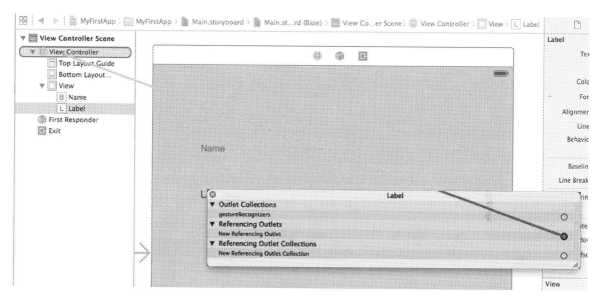

Figure 6-24. *Connecting the referencing outlet to the object*

Once the connection is dropped on the File's Owner icon, a list of outlets in your ViewController object will be displayed, as shown in Figure 6-25. Of the two choices, you want to choose nameLabel. This is the name of the variable in the ViewController object you are using.

Figure 6-25. *Selecting the object's variable to complete the connection*

Once you've chosen nameLabel, you're ready to run your program. Click the Run button (which looks like a Play button) at the top-left corner of the Xcode window (see Figure 6-6). This will automatically save your files and start the application in the iPhone Simulator, as shown in Figure 6-26.

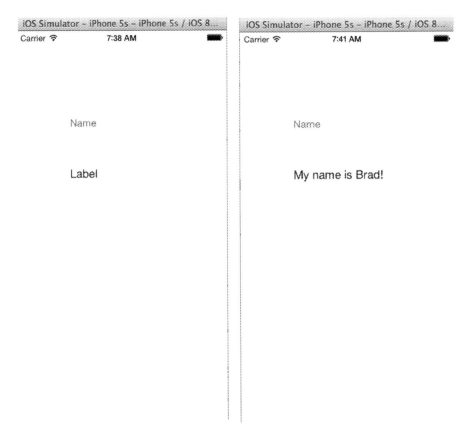

Figure 6-26. The app running, before and after the button is clicked

By clicking the Name button, the Label's text will change from its default value of "Label" to "My Name is Brad!" or whatever value you entered. If you want, go back into the interface and clear the default Label text.

Summary

The examples in this chapter were simple, but ideally they've whetted your appetite for more complex applications using Swift and Xcode. In later chapters, you can expect to learn more about object-oriented programming and more about what Swift can do. Pat yourself on the back because you've learned a lot already. Here is a summary of the topics discussed in this chapter:

- The origins and brief history of the Swift language

- Some common language symbols used in Swift

- A Swift class example

- Using Xcode a bit more, including entering and compiling the HelloWorld.swift source file

- Connecting visual interface objects with methods and variables in your application object

Exercises

- Clear the default text of "Label" in the program and rerun the example.

- Change the size of the Label object on the interface to be smaller in width. How does that affect your text message?

- Delete the referencing outlet connection of the Label and rerun the project. What happens?

- If you think you have the hang of this, add a new Button and Label both to the ViewController object and to the interface. Change the Label from displaying your name to displaying something else.

Chapter 7

Swift Classes, Objects, and Methods

If you haven't already read Chapter 6, please do so before reading this one because it provides a great introduction to some of the basics of Swift. This chapter builds on that foundation. By the end of this chapter, you can expect to have a greater understanding of the Swift language and how to use the basics to write simple programs. The best way to learn is to take small programs and write (or rewrite) them in Swift just to see how the language works.

This chapter will cover what composes a Swift class and how to interact with Swift objects via methods. It will use a simple radio station class as an example of how a Swift class is written. This will impart an understanding of how to use a Swift class. This chapter will also teach you how to formulate a design for objects that are needed to solve a problem. The chapter will touch on how to create custom objects, as well as how to use existing objects provided in the Foundation classes.

This chapter will expand on Chapter 6's topics and incorporate some of the concepts described in detail in Chapter 8.

Creating a Swift Class

Classes are simple to create in Swift. Generally a class will be contained in its own file, but a single file can hold many classes if desired.

Here is a sample of the first line from a class's declaration:

```
class RadioStation
```

Here, the class name is RadioStation. Swift classes, by default, do not inherit from a superclass. If you want to make your Swift class inherit from another class, you can do this like so:

```
class RadioStation: Station
```

In this example, RadioStation is now a subclass of Station and will inherit all of the properties and methods of Station. Listing 7-1 shows the full definition of a class.

Listing 7-1. A Swift Class

```
 1 import UIKit
 2
 3 class RadioStation {
 4
 5     var name: String
 6     var frequency: Double
 7
 8     init() {
 9         name="Default"
10         frequency=100
11     }
12
13     class func minAMFrequency() -> Double {
14         return 520.0
15     }
16
17     class func maxAMFrequency() -> Double {
18         return 1610.0
19     }
20
21     class func minFMFrequency() -> Double {
22         return 88.3
23     }
24
25     class func maxFMFrequency() -> Double {
26         return 107.9
27     }
28
29     func band() ->Int {
30         if frequency >= RadioStation.minFMFrequency() && myStation.frequency <= RadioStation.
           maxFMFrequency() {
31             return 1 //FM
32         } else {
33             return 0 //AM
34         }
35     }
36
37 }
```

Instance Variables

Listing 7-1 shows a sample class with two different properties: name and frequency. Line 1 imports the Foundation class definitions (more on that in a bit). Line 3 starts the definition of the class by defining its name (sometimes called the *type*). Lines 5 to 6 define the properties for the RadioStation class.

Whenever the RadioStation class is instantiated, the resulting RadioStation object has access to these properties, which are only for specific instances. If there are ten RadioStation objects, each object has its own variables independent of the other objects. This is also referred to as *scope*, in that the object's variables are within the scope of each object.

Methods

Almost every object has methods. In Swift, the common concept to interact with an object is calling a method on an object, like so:

```
myStation.band()
```

The preceding line will call a method on an instance of the RadioStation class named myStation.

Methods can also have parameters passed along with them. Why pass parameters? Parameters are passed for several reasons. First (and most common), the range of possibilities is too large to write as separate methods. Second, the data you need to store in your object is variable—like a radio station's name. In the following example, you will see that it isn't practical to write a method for every possible radio frequency; instead, the frequency is passed as a parameter. The same applies to the station name.

```
myStation.setFrequency(104.7)
```

The method name is setFrequency. Method calls can have several parameters, as the following example illustrates:

```
myStation = RationStation.init(name: "KZZP", frequency: 104.7)
```

In the preceding example, the method call consists of two parameters: the station name and its frequency. What's interesting about Swift relative to other languages is that the methods are essentially named parameters. If this were a C++ or Java program, the call would be as follows:

```
myObject = new RadioStation("KZZP", 104.7);
```

While a RadioStation object's parameters might seem obvious, having named parameters can be a bonus because they more or less state what the parameters are used for or what they do.

Using Class Methods

A class doesn't have to be instantiated to be used. In some cases, classes have methods that can actually perform some simple operations and return values. These methods are called *class methods*. In Listing 7-1, the method names that start with class are class methods.

Class methods have limitations. One of their biggest limitations is that none of the instance variables can be used. Being unable to use instance variables makes sense since you haven't instantiated anything. A class method can have its own local variables within the method itself but can't use any of the variables defined as instance variables.

A call to a class method would look like this:

RadioStation.minAMFrequency()

Notice that the call is similar to how a method is called on an instantiated object. The big difference is that instead of an instance variable, the *class name* is used. Class methods are used quite extensively in the Mac OS X and iOS frameworks. They are used mostly for returning some fixed or well-known type of value or to return a new instance of an object. These types of class methods are referred to as *initializers*. Here are some initializer method examples:

```
1.  NSDate.timeIntervalSinceReferenceDate() // Returns a number
2.  NSString(format:"http://%@", "1000")    // Returns a new NSString object
3.  Dictionary<String, String>()            // Returns a new Dictionary object.
```

All of the preceding messages are class methods being called.

Line 1 simply returns a value that represents the number of seconds since January 1, 2001, which is the reference date.

Line 2 returns a new NSString object that has been formatted and has a value of 1000.

Line 3 is a form that is commonly used because it actually allocates a new object. Typically, the line is not used by itself but in a line, like this:

```
var myDict = Dictionary<String, String>()
```

So, when would you use a class method? As a general rule, if the method returns information that is *not* specific to any particular instance of the class, make the method a class method. For example, the minAMFrequency in the preceding example would be the same for all instances of any RadioStation object—this is a great candidate for a class method. However, the station's name or its assigned frequency would be different for each instance of the class. These should not (and indeed could not) be class methods. The reason for this is that class methods cannot use any of the instance variables defined by the class.

Using Instance Methods

Instance methods (lines 29 to 35 in Listing 7-1) are methods that are available only once a class has been instantiated. Here's an example:

```
1 var myStation: RadioStation       // This declares a variable to hold the RadioStation Object.
2 myStation = RadioStation()        // This creates a new object
3 var band = myStation.band()       // This method returns the Band of the Station
4
5
```

Line 3 calls a method on the RadioStation object. The method band returns a 1 for FM and a 0 for AM. An instance method is any method that does not contain the class declaration before it.

Using Your New Class

You've created a simple RadioStation class, but by itself it doesn't accomplish a whole lot. In this section, you will create the Radio class and have it maintain a list of RadioStation classes.

Creating Your Project

Let's start Xcode (see Figure 7-1) and create a new project named RadioStations.

Figure 7-1. Open Xcode so you can create a new project

1. Launch Xcode and select "Create a new Xcode project."

2. Make sure you choose an iOS application and select the Single View Application template, as shown in Figure 7-2.

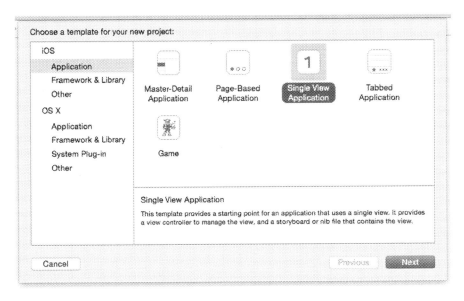

Figure 7-2. Selecting a template in the new project window

3.   Once you've selected the template, click the Next button.

4.   Set the product name (application name) to **RadioStations**.

5.   Set the company identifier (a pretend company will do) and set the device
      family to iPhone (as shown in Figure 7-3). Make sure Swift is selected in the
      Language drop-down list.

Figure 7-3. Naming the new iPhone application

6. Click the Next button, and Xcode will ask you where you want to save your new project. You can save the project on your desktop or anywhere in your home folder. Once you've made your choice, simply click the Create button.

7. Once you've clicked the Create button, the Xcode workspace window should be visible, as shown in Figure 7-4.

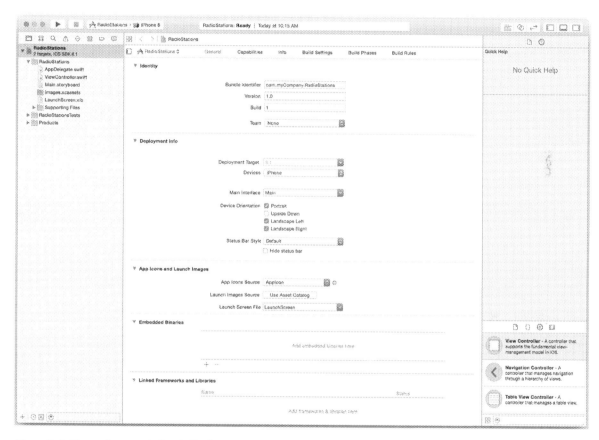

Figure 7-4. *The workspace window in Xcode*

Adding Objects

Now you can add your new objects.

1. First, create your RadioStation object. Right-click the RadioStations group folder and select New File (as shown in Figure 7-5).

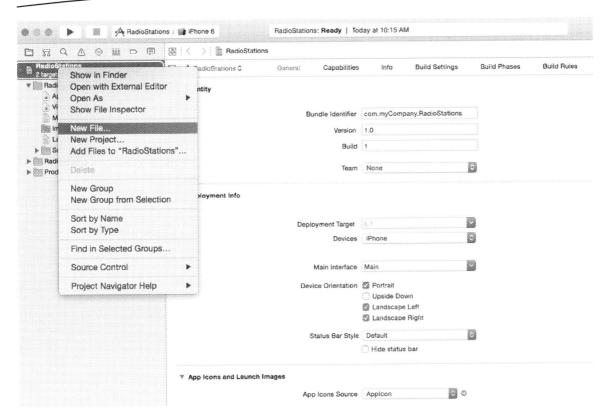

Figure 7-5. Adding a new file

2. The next screen, shown in Figure 7-6, asks for the new file type. Simply choose Swift File from the Source group, and then click Next.

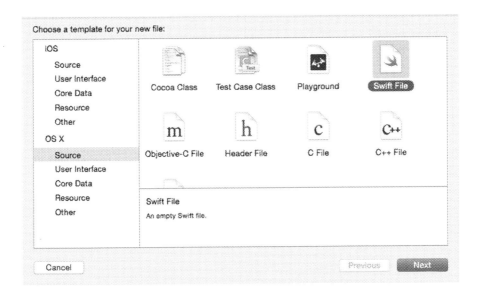

Figure 7-6. Selecting the new file type

3. The next screen asks you where to create the files and what you want to name the file. Enter **RadioStation** for the file name, and then simply click the Create button, since the location in which Xcode chooses to save the files is within the current project, as shown in Figure 7-7.

Figure 7-7. Choosing where to create your new files

4. Your project window should now look like Figure 7-8. Click the RadioStation.swift file. Notice that the stub of your new RadioStation class is already present. Now, fill in the empty class so it looks like Listing 7-1, your RadioStation Swift file.

Figure 7-8. Your newly created file in the workspace window

Writing the Class

Now that you have created your project and your new RadioStation.swift file, you are ready to begin creating your class.

1. The class file you'll use here has been simplified a bit from the example several pages ago but will work perfectly for the radio station application. Click the RadioStation.swift file, and enter the code in your class, as shown in Figure 7-9.

```
//
//  RadioStation.swift
//  RadioStations
//
//  Created by Thorn on 10/28/14.
//  Copyright (c) 2014 inn. All rights reserved.
//

import UIKit

class RadioStation {


    var name: String
    var frequency: Double




    init() {
        name="Default"
        frequency=100
    }

    class func minAMFrequency() -> Double {
        return 520.0
    }

    class func maxAMFrequency() -> Double {
        return 1610.0
    }

    class func minFMFrequency() -> Double {
        return 88.3
    }

    class func maxFMFrequency() -> Double {
        return 107.9
    }

    func band() ->Int {
        if frequency >= RadioStation.minFMFrequency() && frequency <= RadioStation.maxFMFrequency() {
            return 1 //FM
        } else {
            return 0 //AM
        }
    }

}
```

Figure 7-9. The RadioStation class file

We will come back to a few items in Figure 7-9 and explain them further in a moment; however, with the RadioStation class defined, you can now write the code that will actually use it.

2. Click the ViewController.swift file. You'll need to define a few variables for this class to use, as shown in Figure 7-10.

```
//
//  ViewController.swift
//  RadioStations
//
//  Created by Thorn on 10/28/14.
//  Copyright (c) 2014 inn. All rights reserved.
//

import UIKit

class ViewController: UIViewController {

    var myStation: RadioStation

    required init(coder aDecoder: NSCoder) {

        myStation = RadioStation()
        myStation.frequency=125.5
        myStation.name = "Knix"
        super.init(coder: aDecoder)
    }

    override func viewDidLoad() {
        super.viewDidLoad()
        // Do any additional setup after loading the view, typically from a nib.
    }

    override func didReceiveMemoryWarning() {
        super.didReceiveMemoryWarning()
        // Dispose of any resources that can be recreated.
    }

}
```

Line 13 defines the variable myStation of type RadioStation. Lines 15 to 21 contain the required init. In Swift, classes do not require an initializer method, but it is a good place to set the default values of your object. This method sets up the variables used in that class. Lines 23 to 25 are going to be used by your iOS interface to show some values on the screen (more on these later). Also, don't forget to include the curly braces ({ … }).

Creating the User Interface

Next, the main window has to be set up in order to display your station information.

1. Click the `Main.storyboard` file. This file produces the main iPhone screen. Click the Object Library icon, as shown in Figure 7-10.

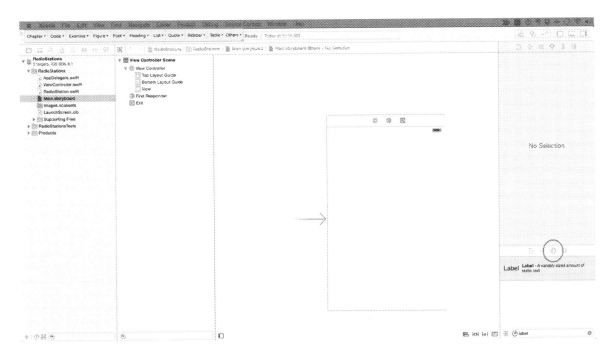

Figure 7-10. Adding a Label object to your iPhone screen

2. Drag and drop three Label objects onto the screen, as shown in Figure 7-11. The labels can be aligned in any manner, or as shown in Figure 7-11.

3. You're going to need space, however. Once the Label objects are on the iPhone screen, double-click each Label object in order to change its text so that the iPhone screen looks something like Figure 7-11.

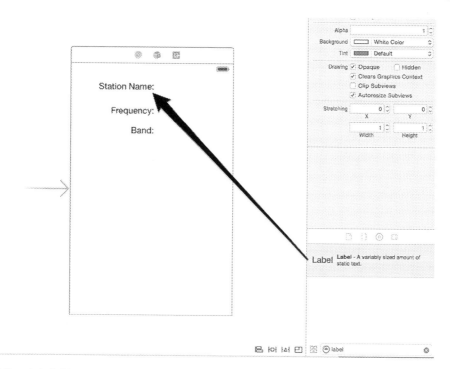

Figure 7-11. All three Label objects on the iPhone screen

4. Next, add a Button object to the screen, as shown in Figure 7-12. This button, when clicked, will cause the screen to be updated with your radio station information.

Figure 7-12. Adding a Button object to the screen

5. Just like with the Label object, simply double-click the Button object in order change its Title to My Station.

6. Next, you need to add the Label fields that will hold the radio station information. These fields are situated just after the existing Label objects, as shown in Figure 7-13. Once the Label object is placed, it needs to be resized so that it extends to the edge of the iPhone screen, as shown in Figure 7-14.

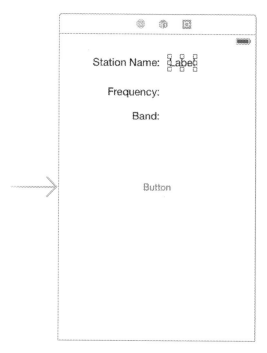

Figure 7-13. *Adding another Label object*

Figure 7-14. *Stretching the Label object*

Note   Stretching the Label object allows the Label's text to contain a reasonably long string. If you didn't resize the Label object, the text would be cut off (since it wouldn't fit), or the font size would get smaller.[1]

7. Repeat adding and sizing a Label object next to the existing Frequency and Band Labels, as shown in Figure 7-15. It's OK to leave the default text of the Label set to "Label" for now.

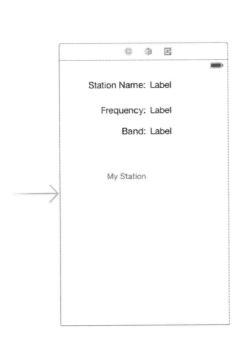

Figure 7-15. Adding another Label object

Hooking Up the Code

Now that all the user interface objects are in place, you can begin to hook up these interface elements to the variables in your program. As you saw in Chapter 6, you do this by *connecting* the user interface objects with the objects in your program.

---

[1]By using either code or Interface Builder, you can customize how the Label object reacts to text that is too large to fit. The behavior described is based upon typical defaults for the Label object.

1. Start by connecting the Label object by station name to your variable, as shown in Figure 7-16. Right-click (or Control-click) the View Controller object and drag it to the Label object next to the "Station Name:" text to bring up the list of outlets.

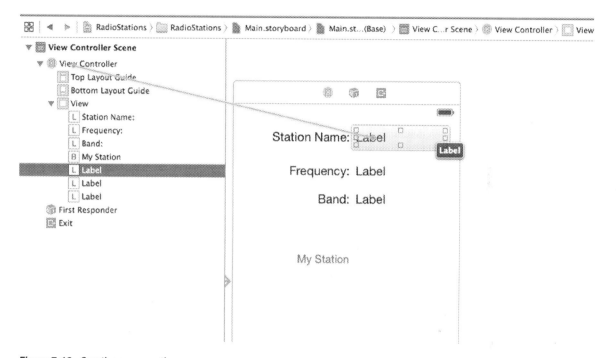

Figure 7-16. Creating a connection

2. When the connection is dropped from the View Controller icon, another small menu will be shown. Click the instance variable name that you want to display in this Label object—in this case, you want the stationName instance variable, as shown in Figure 7-17.

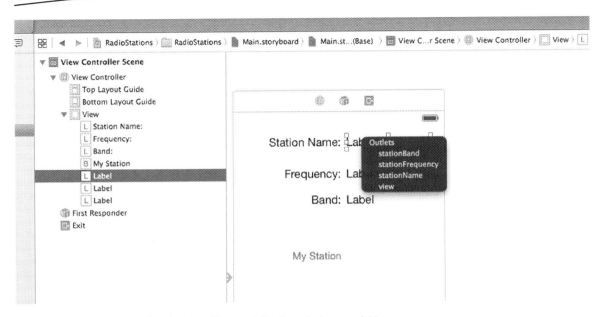

Figure 7-17. *Connecting the interface Label to your stationName instance variable*

3.   Now, the interface Label object is *connected* to the stationName instance
     variable. Whenever you set the instance variable's value, the screen will also
     be updated. Repeat the previous connection steps for Frequency and Band.

To hook up your button, you need a method in the ViewController class to handle this. You could
go to the ViewController.swift file and add it there. There is also a shortcut to adding @IBOutlet
methods. In the Xcode toolbar, click the Assistant Editor icon shown in Figure 7-18 (it looks like a
two circles or a tuxedo in Mavericks).

Figure 7-18. *The Assistant Editor icon*

After clicking the Assistant Editor icon, a second window will pop open showing the ViewController
source. Right-click and drag the button to the code window, as shown in Figure 7-19.

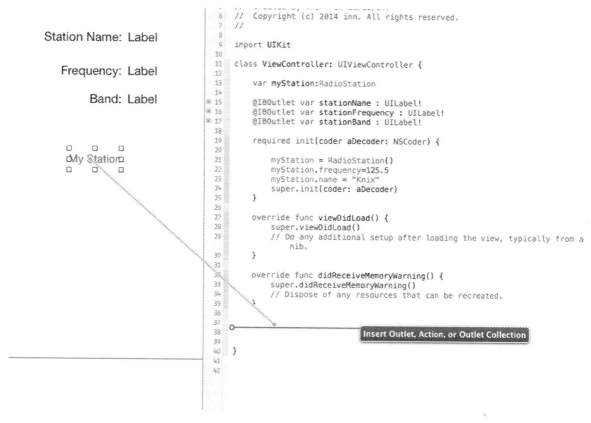

```
   6    //  Copyright (c) 2014 inn. All rights reserved.
   7    //
   8
   9    import UIKit
  10
  11    class ViewController: UIViewController {
  12
  13        var myStation:RadioStation
  14
  15        @IBOutlet var stationName : UILabel!
  16        @IBOutlet var stationFrequency : UILabel!
  17        @IBOutlet var stationBand : UILabel!
  18
  19        required init(coder aDecoder: NSCoder) {
  20
  21            myStation = RadioStation()
  22            myStation.frequency=125.5
  23            myStation.name = "Knix"
  24            super.init(coder: aDecoder)
  25        }
  26
  27        override func viewDidLoad() {
  28            super.viewDidLoad()
  29            // Do any additional setup after loading the view, typically from a
                      nib.
  30        }
  31
  32        override func didReceiveMemoryWarning() {
  33            super.didReceiveMemoryWarning()
  34            // Dispose of any resources that can be recreated.
  35        }
  36
  37
  38                                            Insert Outlet, Action, or Outlet Collection
  39
  40    }
  41
  42
```

Station Name: Label

Frequency: Label

Band: Label

My Station

Figure 7-19. Using Assistant Editor to create your method

4. When you release the mouse, a little window will pop up, as shown in Figure 7-20.

Figure 7-20. Creating the action

Select Action and set the name to buttonClick. Xcode will now create your method for you.

Finish your method by adding the code shown in Figure 7-21.

```
37    @IBAction func buttonClick(sender: AnyObject) {
38        stationName.text = myStation.name
39        stationFrequency.text = String(format:"%f", myStation.frequency)
40
41        if myStation.frequency >= RadioStation.minFMFrequency() &&
    myStation.frequency <= RadioStation.maxFMFrequency() {
42            stationBand.text = "FM"
43        } else {
44            stationBand.text = "AM"
45        }
46
47    }
```

Figure 7-21. Finished buttonClick method

Let's walk through the code you just added. First, on line 37, you'll notice the IBAction type. This lets Xcode know that this method can be called as a result of an action. So, when you go to connect an action to your application, you will see this method.

Line 38 and line 39 both set the text fields to the values found in your RadioStation class. Line 38 is as follows:

stationName.text = myStation.name

The stationName variable is what you just connected to the user interface Label object, and myStation.name is used to return the name of the station.

Line 39 effectively does the same thing as line 38, but you have to first convert the double value (the station's frequency) to an NSString. The @"%.1f means that you convert a floating-point value and should see only one digit after the decimal point.

Lines 41 to 45 make use of both the instance variables and the class methods of the RadioStation class. Here, you simply check to see whether the frequency of the radio station is between minFMFrequency and maxFMFrequency. If so, the station is an FM station; otherwise, assume it's the AM band. Lines 8 and 10 will show the band value on the screen.

> **Tip** The Button sends the Touch Up Inside event whenever a user touches the *inside* of the button and then releases—not until the user lifts his or her finger does the event actually get sent.

Running the Program

Once the connection has been made, you're ready to run and test your program! To do this, simply click the Run button at the top left of the Xcode window, as shown in Figure 7-22.

Figure 7-22. Click the Play button to run your program

If there are no compile errors, the iPhone Simulator should come up, and you should see your application. Simply click the My Station button, and the radio station information will be displayed, as shown in Figure 7-23.

Figure 7-23. Showing your radio station information

If things don't quite look or work right, retrace your steps and make sure all the code and connections are in place as described in this chapter.

Taking Class Methods to the Next Level

In your program, you haven't taken advantage of all the class methods for RadioStation, but this chapter does describe what a class method is and how it is used. Use that knowledge to try a few of the exercises mentioned at the end of this chapter. Just play around with this simple working program by adding or changing class or instance methods to get an idea of how they work.

Accessing the Xcode Documentation

There is a wealth of information provided in the Xcode developer documentation . When Xcode is opened, choose Help ➤ Documentation and API Reference (see Figure 7-24) to open the Documentation window.

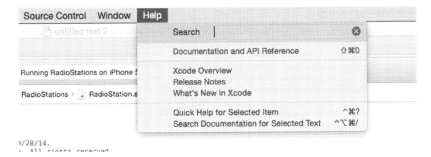

Figure 7-24. The Xcode Help menu

Once opened, the search window can be used to look up any of the Swift classes you've used in this chapter, including the String class documentation, as shown in Figure 7-25.

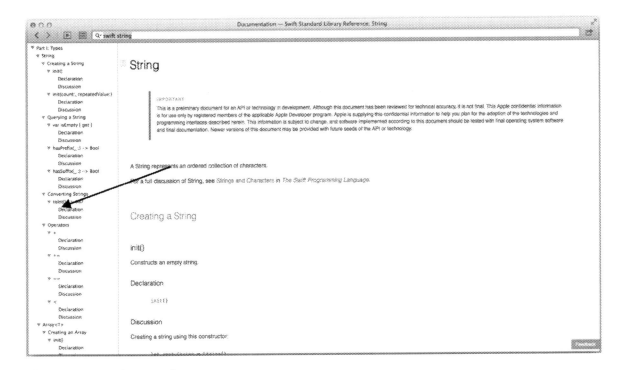

Figure 7-25. Xcode documentation

There are several different things to discover about the String class shown in Figure 7-25. Go through the documentation and the various companion guides that Apple provides. This will give you a more thorough understanding of the various classes and the various methods supported by them.

Summary

Once again, congratulate yourself for being able to single-handedly stuff your brain with a lot of information! Here is a summary of what was covered in this chapter:

- Swift classes review
  - Class methods
  - Instance methods
- Creating a class
  - Limitations of using class methods versus instance methods
  - Initializing the class and making use of the instance variables
- Making use of your new RadioStation object
  - Building an iPhone app that uses your new object
  - Connecting interface classes to instance variables
  - Connecting user interface events to methods in your class

Exercises

- Change the code that creates your RadioStation class and make the station's name much longer than what can appear on the screen. What happens?
- Change the current button and add a new button. Label the buttons FM and AM. If the user clicks the FM button, show an FM station. If the user clicks the AM button, display an AM station (hint: you'll need to add a second RadioStation object to the ViewController.swift file).
- Clean up the interface a little by making sure that the user doesn't see the text "Label" when the iPhone application first starts.
  - Fix the issue by using the interface tool.
  - How could you fix this by adding code to the application instead?
- Add more validation to the @IBAction func buttonClick(sender: AnyObject) method. Right now, it validates FM ranges but not AM ranges. Fix the code so that it also validates an AM range.
  - If the radio station frequency is out of bounds, use the existing Labels to display some type of error message.

Chapter 8

Programming Basics in Swift

Swift is an elegant language. It mixes the efficiency of a compiled language with the flexibility and modern features of many scripting languages.

This chapter introduces some of the more common concepts of Swift, such as properties and collection classes. It also shows how properties and instance variables are used from within Xcode when dealing with user interface elements. This sounds like a lot to accomplish, but Swift, the Foundation framework, and the Xcode tool provide a wealth of objects and methods and a way to build applications with ease.

Using let vs. var

If you have spent much time with Swift, you have seen the word `var` appear before variable declarations. You may also have seen `let` before other declarations. The word `var` is used to define a variable, while the word `let` is used to define a constant. This means that if you declare a value with `let`, you will not be able to change the value. The following code defines a constant:

```
let myName = "Brad"
```

Once you define a constant, you cannot change the value.

```
myName = "John"
```

This will give you an error. It you want to create a mutable or changeable variable, you need to use `var`. For example, you can do the following:

```
var myName = "Brad"
```

```
myName = "John"
```

This will not give you any errors because myName is now a variable. This does not relate to only Strings and Ints, but it can also be used with collections and other more complex objects.

Because variables give you more flexibility, why would anyone ever want to use a constant? The quick answer is performance. If you know that you have a value that will not change, the compiler can optimize that value as a constant.

Understanding Collections

Understanding collections is a fundamental part of learning Swift. In fact, collection objects are fundamental constructs of nearly every modern object-oriented language library (sometimes they are referred to as *containers*). Simply put, a *collection* is a type of class that can hold and manage other objects. The whole purpose of a collection is that it provides a common way to store and retrieve objects efficiently.

There are several types of collections. While they all fulfill the same purpose of being able to hold other objects, they differ mostly in the way objects are retrieved. The most common collections used in Swift are the array and the dictionary.

Both of these collections can be created as constants or regular variables. If you create a collection as a constant, you must fill it with the objects at the time of creation. It cannot be modified after that point.

Using Array

The Array class is like any other collection, in that it allows the programmer to manage a group of objects. An array is an *ordered* collection, which means that objects are entered in an array in a certain order and retrieved in the same order.

> **Note**   There are some methods for working with arrays that allow you to change the order of the objects or to add an object at a specific location in the array.

The Array class allows an object to be retrieved by its *index* into the array. An index is the numeric position that an object would occupy in the array. For example, if there are three elements in the array, the objects can be referenced with an index from 0 to 2. Like with most things in Swift and other programming languages, an index starts at 0, not 1. See listing 8-1.

Listing 8-1. Accessing Objects Within an Array

```
1    var myArray:  [String]= ["One", "Two", "Three"]
2    println (myArray[0])
3    println (myArray[1])
4    println (myArray[2]);
```

As you can see, objects within the array can be retrieved via the index. The index starts at 0 and can't exceed the size of the array minus 1. You can easily calculate the size of the array by sending a count message to the Array object, as shown here:

```
var entries = myArray.count
```

In fact, every collection type, in other words, Array and Dictionary, will respond to the count message.

Adding items to the end of an array is simple. You can just call the append method on the array. See Listing 8-2.

Listing 8-2. Adding Objects to an Array

```
1    var myArray: [String] = ["One", "Two", "Three"]
2    myArray.append("Four")
3    myArray.append("Five")
4    myArray.append("Six")
```

Swift provides you with many different methods for adding items to an array. If you want to add multiple objects to an array, you can use the standard += (often called *plus equals*) operator. Listing 8-3 creates an array and then adds three more String objects to the array on line 2. Notice the new values are in brackets instead of parentheses.

Listing 8-3. Adding Multiple Objects to an Array

```
1    var myArray: [String] = ["One", "Two", "Three"]
2    myArray += ["Four", "Five", "Six"]
```

As discussed earlier, an array is actually ordered. The order of the objects in your array is important. There may be times where you need to add an item at a certain position in the array. You can accomplish this with the insert(atIndex:) method, as shown in Listing 8-4.

Listing 8-4. Adding a String to the Beginning of an Array

```
1    var myArray: [String] = ["Two", "Three"]
2    myArray.insert("One", atIndex:0)
```

The array now contains One, Two, Three.

Accessing items in an array is simple. You can use standard square brackets to access an object at a certain position. For example, myArray[0] would give you the first object in the array. If you want to loop through each of the items in the array, you can use something called *fast enumeration*. Listing 8-5 is an example of fast enumeration.

Listing 8-5. Fast Enumeration

```
1    var myArray: [String] = ["One", "Two", "Three"]
2    for myString in myArray {
3        println(myString)
4    }
5
```

The magic happens in line 2 of Listing 8-5. You tell Swift to assign each value of myArray to a new variable called myString. You can then do whatever you want to do with myString. In this case, you just print it. It will go through all of the objects in the array without you having to know the total number of objects. This is a fast and effective way to pull items out of an array.

Removing objects from an array is simple too. You can use the removeAtIndex method, as shown in Listing 8-6.

Listing 8-6. Removing an Object

```
1    var myArray: [String] = ["One", "Two", "Three"]
2    myArray.removeAtIndex(1)
3    for myString in myArray {
4        println(myString)
5    }
```

The output from Listing 8-6 will be One, Three. This is because you removed the object with the index of 1. Remember, this is the second object in the array because array indexes always begin at 0.

You have seen how flexible Swift is in letting you interact with arrays. They are powerful collections that you will use on a regular basis as a programmer. This section covered the basics of arrays, but there are many more things arrays can do.

Dictionary

The Swift Dictionary class is also a useful type of collection class. It allows the storage of objects, just like the Array class, but Dictionary is different in that it allows a *key* to be associated with the entry. For example, you could create a dictionary that stores a list of attributes about someone such as a firstName, lastName, and so on. Instead of accessing the attributes with an index like with an array, the dictionary could use a String like "firstName". However, all keys must be unique—that is, "firstName" cannot exist more than once. Depending on your program, finding unique names is normally not a problem.

Here's an example of how you create a dictionary:

```
var person: [String: String] = ["firstName": "John", "lastName": "Doe"]
```

This creates a simple dictionary called person. The next part of the declaration tells the dictionary what kinds of objects the keys and the values will be. In this case, the keys are Strings, and the values are Strings. You then add two keys to the dictionary. The first key is firstName, and that key has a value of John. The second key is lastName, and that has a value of Doe. You can access the values in the dictionary by using a similar notation to arrays.

```
println(person["firstName"])
```

This code will print the name Optional("John") since that is the value for the key firstName. The Optional appears in the previous example because the value of a key in a dictionary is an optional value. You can use the same style of code to change the values in a dictionary. Let's say, for this example, that John now likes to go by Joe instead. You can change the value in the dictionary with a simple line of code.

```
person["firstName"] = "Joe"
```

You can add a new key to a dictionary with the same notation.

```
person["gender"] = "Male"
```

If you decide you want to remove a key from a dictionary, such as the gender key you just added, you can do so by setting the key to nil.

```
person["gender"] = nil
```

Now the dictionary will contain only firstName and lastName. Remember that dictionaries are not ordered. You cannot rely on the order, but there will be times when you need to iterate over a dictionary. This is done in a manner similar to arrays. The main difference is that in an array, you assign one variable, while in a dictionary, you need to assign the key and the value. See Listing 8-7.

Listing 8-7. Iterating Over a Dictionary

```
1    var person: [String: String] = ["firstName": "John", "lastName": "Doe"]
2    for (myKey,myValue) in person {
3        println(myKey + ": " + myValue)
4    }
```

This example will print the following:

```
firstName: John
lastName: Doe
```

Dictionaries are a great way to organize data that does not need to be ordered. It is also a great way to look up data based on a certain key. They are very flexible in Swift and should be used to organize and optimize your code.

Creating the BookStore Application

You are going to create an app that will demonstrate how to use arrays. You will create a UITableView and use an array to populate the UITableView with data. Let's start by creating the base application project. Open Xcode and select a new Master-Detail Application project, as shown in Figure 8-1. In this project, you will create a few simple objects for what is to become your bookstore application: a Book object and the BookStore object. You'll visit instance variables again and see how to get and set the value of one during this project. Lastly, you'll put the bookstore objects to use, and you'll learn how to make use of objects once you've created them.

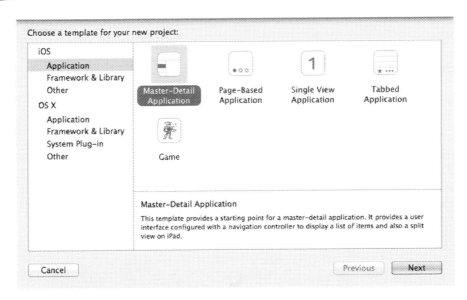

Figure 8-1. Creating the initial project based on the Master-Detail Application template

1. Click the Next button, and name the project **BookStore**, as shown in
    Figure 8-2. The company name is required—you can use any company
    name, real or otherwise. The example uses com.mycompany, which is
    perfectly fine. Make sure the device family is iPhone and that the language is
    set to Swift. Do not check the Use Core Data check box.

Figure 8-2. Selecting the product (application) name and options

Note   This type of app would be a good candidate for using Core Data, but Core Data is not introduced until Chapter 11. You will use an array for data storage in this app.

2.   Once everything is filled out, click the Next button. Xcode will prompt you to specify a place to save the project. Anywhere you can remember is fine—the desktop is a good place.

3.   Once you decide on a location, click the Create button to create the new project. This will create the boilerplate BookStore project, as shown in Figure 8-3.

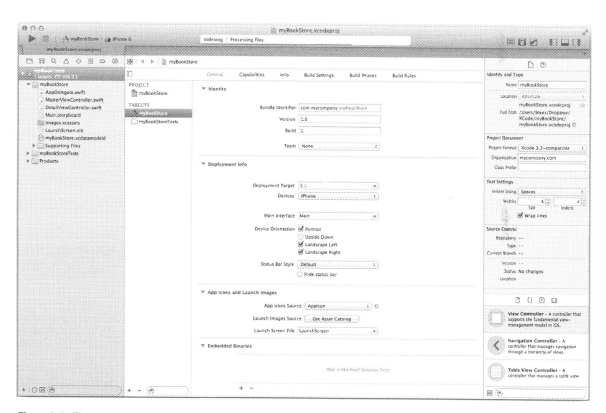

Figure 8-3. The source listing of the boilerplate project

4.   Click the plus (+) sign at the lower left of the screen in the Navigator area to add a new object to the project. Click New File. Then choose Source under the iOS section on the left and choose Swift File on the right, as shown in Figure 8-4. It's also possible to right-click (or Control-click) the Navigation area and then select the New File menu option. There is no difference between this approach and clicking the plus sign—do whatever feels more natural.

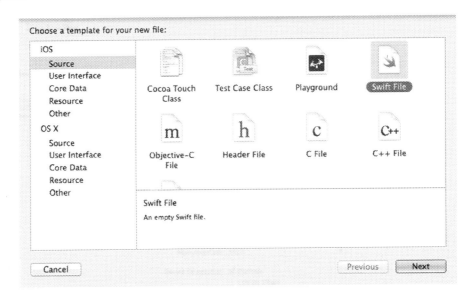

Figure 8-4. Creating a new Swift file

5. You're choosing a plain Swift file, which will create a new empty Swift file that you're going to use for the Book class. After selecting this, click the Next button.

6. Xcode will ask you what to name your file. Use the name Book. Xcode will also ask to which folder it should save the new file. To keep things simple, choose the MyBookstore folder in your project, as shown in Figure 8-5. This is where all the other class files for the project are stored.

Figure 8-5. Choosing the name and place to save the new class files

7.   Double-click the MyBookstore folder and then click the Create button. You'll see the main edit window for Xcode and the new file, Book.swift, in the Navigator area, as shown in Figure 8-6.

Figure 8-6. The empty Swift file

8. Repeat the previous steps and create a second object called `Bookstore`.
    This will create a `Bookstore.swift` file. You'll be using this class later in this
    chapter. For now, you'll concentrate on the `Book` class.

9. Click the `Book.swift` file and let's start defining your new class!

Creating Your Class

You will notice that Xcode does not give you a new class when you create a Swift file. In Objective-C,
Xcode used to create the `.h` and `.m` files for you. Swift is more flexible, and it is not necessary to
have only one class per file. Xcode allows you to add the classes as you want.

> **Note**   It is still a good idea to keep your Swift classes in separate files. This makes organizing and finding
> classes easier, especially when dealing with large projects.

Let's create the Book class. Type the following code into the `Book.swift` file:

```
class Book {

}
```

Now you have your class, as shown in Figure 8-7. That is all you need to do to create a class.

```
 1   //
 2   //  BookStore.swift
 3   //  myBookStore
 4   //
 5   //  Created by Brad Lees on 11/9/14.
 6   //  Copyright (c) 2014 mycompany.com. All rights reserved.
 7   //
 8
 9   import Foundation
10
11   class Book {
12
13   }
14
15
```

Figure 8-7. *The empty Book class*

Introducing Instance Variables

The class is simply called Book. True, you have an class, but it doesn't *store* anything at this point. For this class to be useful, it needs to be able to hold some information, which is done with instance variables. When an object is used, it has to be instantiated. Once the object is instantiated, it has access to its instance variables. These variables are available to the object as long as the object stays in scope. As you know from Chapter 7, scope defines the context in which an object exists. In some cases, an object's scope may be the life of the program. In other cases, the scope might be just a function or method. It all depends on where the object is declared and how it's used. Scope will be discussed more later. For now, let's add some instance variables to the Book class to make it more useful.

Listing 8-8. Adding Instance Variables to the Book.h File

```
1    //
2    //  Book.swift
3    //  myBookStore
4    //
5    //  Created by Thorn on 11/9/14.
6    //  Copyright (c) 2014 mycompany.com. All rights reserved.
7    //
8
9    import Foundation
10    class Book {
11        var title: String = ""
12        var author: String = ""
13        var description: String = ""
14
15    }
```

Listing 8-8 shows the same `Book` object from before, but now there are three new instance variables placed inside the brackets, on lines 11 to 13. These are all `String` objects, which means they can hold text information for the `Book` object. So, the `Book` object now has a place to store title, author, and description information.

Accessing Variables

Now that you have some instance variables, how can you use them? How are they accessed? As you learned in previous chapters, Swift objects respond to messages. Unfortunately, simply declaring an instance variable doesn't necessarily give you access to it. There are two ways to access these variables.

- ▓ One way is, of course, within the Book object.

- ▓ The second way is from outside the object—that is, another part of the program that uses the Book object.

If you are writing the code for a method within the `Book` object, accessing an instance variable is quite simple. For example, you could simply write the following:

```
title = "Test Title"
```

From outside the object, you can still access the `title` variable. This is done through the use of dot notation.

```
myBookObject.title = "Test Title"
```

Finishing the Bookstore Program

With the understanding of instance variables and properties, you are going to now venture forth to create the actual bookstore program. The idea is simple enough—create a class called `Bookstore` that will be stocked with a few `Book` objects.

Creating the View

Let's start by first getting the view ready. If you need a refresher on how to build an interface in Xcode, please refer to Chapter 6.

1.   Click the `Main.storyboard` file in the Navigator area. You will see three scenes in the `Main.storyboard` file. Navigate to the right to find the detail scene. This will display Xcode's Interface Builder, as shown in Figure 8-8.

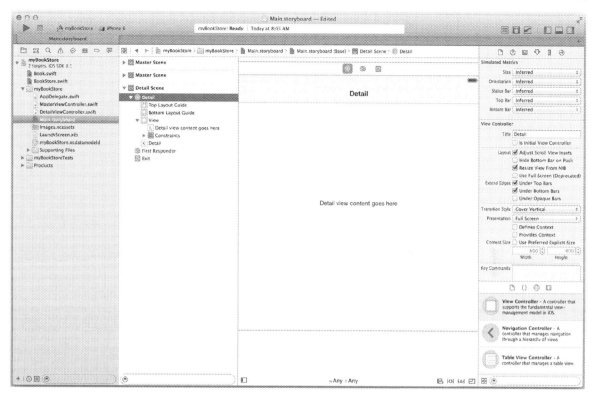

Figure 8-8. Preparing the Bookstore detail view

2. By default, when you create a blank master-detail app, Xcode adds a Label with the text "Detail view content goes here." Select and delete this Label object because you are going to add your own. You're going to add some new fields to display some details about a selected book. Since you deleted this control, you also need to remove the code that references it.

    a. In the DetailViewController.swift file, remove the following line:

    ```
    @IBOutlet weak var detailDescriptionLabel: UILabel!
    ```

    b. In the var detailItem: AnyObject? method, remove the following line:

    ```
    self.configureView()
    ```

    c. In the DetailViewController.swift file, in the method named configureView, remove the following lines:

    ```
    // Update the user interface for the detail item.
    if let detail: AnyObject = self.detailItem {
        if let label = self.detailDescriptionLabel {
            label.text = detail.valueForKey("timeStamp")!.description
        }
    }
    ```

Your DetailViewController.swift file should now look like Figure 8-9.

Figure 8-9. Modified DetailViewController

    3.   Drag some Label objects from the Object Library onto the detail view, as shown in Figure 8-10. Make sure that the lower Label controls are set to the width of the view. This is so that they can hold a fairly large amount of text. The two Label objects with the text "Label" in them are the ones you're going to hook up to hold two of the values from the Book object: Title and Author.

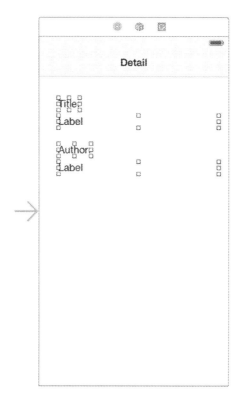

Figure 8-10. Adding some Label objects

Adding Instance Variables

Next, you'll add some instance variables to the `DetailViewController` class. These instance variables will correspond to the detail view's Label objects.

1. Click the Assistant Editor icon (it looks like two circles) in the top-right corner of Xcode to open the Assistant editor.

2. Hold the Control key and drag the first blank Label control to the code on the right side, as shown in Figure 8-11. Name the first one `titleLabel` (see Figure 8-12) and then repeat the process with the second one and name it `authorLabel`. This will add two variables to your `DetailViewController` class, as seen in Listing 8-9, and hook them up to the Label controls in the interface.

Figure 8-11. Creating variables

Figure 8-12. Naming the new variable

Listing 8-9. Modifying the DetailViewController.swift File to Include the New Labels

```
1        @IBOutlet weak var titleLabel: UILabel!
2        @IBOutlet weak var authorLabel: UILabel!
```

Adding a Description

Now you need to add the description to the view. The description is a little different in that it can span multiple lines. For this, you're going to use the Text View object.

1. Start by adding "Description:" text to the view, as shown in Figure 8-13.

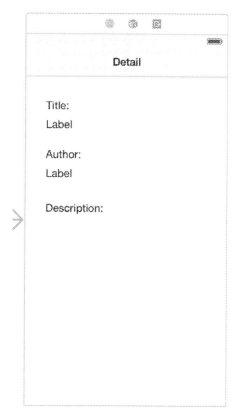

Figure 8-13. Adding a new Label object for the description

2. Next, add the Text View object to the detail view, as shown in Figure 8-14. The advantage the Text View object has is that it's easy to display multiple lines of text. While the Label object can display multiple lines, it's not as clean as the Text View object.

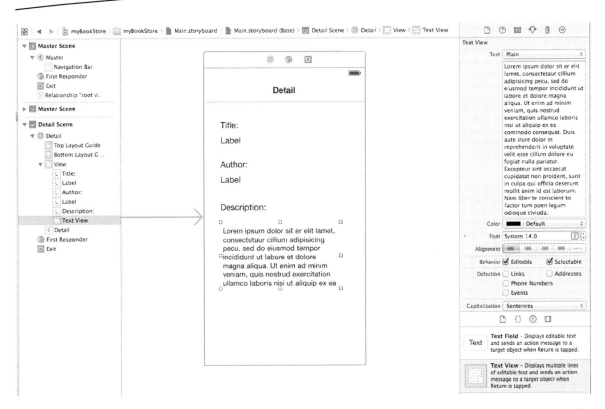

Figure 8-14. *Adding a Text View to the detail view*

Note   By default, the Text View control is filled with all kinds of seemingly random text. This text is called *Lorem Ipsum* text. If you ever need to fill up a page with text, you can find any number of Lorem Ipsum generators on the Web. As for the Text View control, the text can stay as it is since you'll remove it during runtime. Plus, if it's cleared, it becomes a little more difficult spotting exactly where the Text View control is on the screen—it's white on white!

3.   For the program to take advantage of the Text View, you'll need to create an outlet for it, just like you did for the title and description. Simply Control-drag the Text View to your `DetailViewController` file, as you did earlier. Name this variable `descriptionTextView`. The finished variable portion of `detailViewController` will look like Listing 8-10.

Listing 8-10. Adding an Outlet for the Text View to Hold a Description

```
1    import UIKit
2
3    class DetailViewController: UIViewController {
4
5        @IBOutlet weak var titleLabel: UILabel!
6        @IBOutlet weak var authorLabel: UILabel!
7
8        @IBOutlet weak var descriptionTextView: UITextView!
```

4.   Notice that the type is UITextView instead of UILabel—this is important.

> **Caution**   As mentioned, it's important to make the descriptionTextView property a UITextView type.
> If, for example, it was accidentally made a UILabel object, when trying to connect the Text View from the
> screen to the outlet, Xcode wouldn't be able to find the descriptionTextView outlet. Why? Xcode knows
> that the control is a UITextView and is looking for an outlet that is of type UITextView.

Creating a Simple Data Model Class

For the application to work, it needs to have some data to display. To do this, you're going to use the
Bookstore object you created earlier as the data model class. There's nothing different about a data
model class except that its whole purpose is to allow an application to access data via an object.

Modify the Bookstore.swift file to look like Listing 8-11.

Listing 8-11. Modifying the Bookstore.swift Class to Include an Array

```
1    //
2    //  BookStore.swift
3    //  myBookStore
4    //
5    //  Created by Thorn on 11/9/14.
6    //  Copyright (c) 2014 mycompany.com. All rights reserved.
7    //
8
9    import Foundation
10
11   class BookStore {
12       var theBookStore: [Book] = []
13   }
```

On line 12, you add a variable that will hold the list of books; the property is simply named
theBookStore. Note that theBookStore is an array, which will allow you to add a series of objects, in
this case, a set of Book objects.

Next, let's add the code to the Swift file, `Bookstore.swift`, as shown in Listing 8-12.

Listing 8-12. Implementing the BookStore Data Object

```
1    //
2    //   BookStore.swift
3    //   myBookStore
4    //
5    //   Created by Thorn on 11/9/14.
6    //   Copyright (c) 2014 mycompany.com. All rights reserved.
7    //
8
9    import Foundation
10
11   class BookStore {
12       var theBookStore: [Book] = []
13
14       init() {
15           var newBook = Book()
16           newBook.title = "Swift for Absolute Beginners"
17           newBook.author = "Bennett and Lees"
18           newBook.description = "iOS Programming made easy."
19           theBookStore.append(newBook)
20
21           newBook = Book()
22           newBook.title = "A Farewell To Arms"
23           newBook.author = "Ernest Hemingway"
24           newBook.description = "The story of an affair between an English nurse and an American
                 soldier on the Italian front during World War I."
25
26           theBookStore.append(newBook)
27
28
29       }
30   }
```

In Listing 8-5, lines 14 to 30 define the `init` method of the object, which is called whenever
the object is first initialized. In this method, you initialize the two books you plan to add to your
bookstore. Line 15 is where the first Book object is allocated and initialized. Lines 16 to 18 add
a title, author, and description to your first book. Finally, line 19 adds the new Book object to the
`theBookStore` array. The important thing to note here is that once the object is added to the array, the
code can forget about it; the array now owns that object. Because of this, line 21 is not a problem.

Line 21 allocates a new Book object overwriting the old value. This tells the compiler that you're no
longer interested in using the old value.

Lines 22 to 26 simply add the second book to the array.

That's it! That's all you need to define a simple data model class. Next, you need to modify
`MasterViewController` to access this class so that it can start displaying some data.

Modifying MasterViewController

The simple application has two view controllers: the main view controller, which is called MasterViewController, and a secondary one called DetailViewController. View controllers are objects that simply control the behavior of a view. For the application to start displaying data from the data model, you need to first modify MasterViewController—this is where the navigation of the application begins. The following code is already in place in the template that Xcode has provided. You're just going to modify it to add in your data model.

First you'll need to modify the MasterViewController.swift file. You need to add a variable to hold the Bookstore object. Listing 8-13 shows that the instance variable is added as a property on line 15.

Listing 8-13. Adding in the Bookstore Object

```
 1 //
 2 //  MasterViewController.swift
 3 //  Chapter 8.1
 4 //
 5 //  Created by Thorn on 11/9/14.
 6 //  Copyright (c) 2014 mycompany.com. All rights reserved.
 7 //
 8
 9 import UIKit
10
11
12 class MasterViewController: UITableViewController {
13
14     var objects = NSMutableArray()
15     var myBookStore: BookStore = BookStore()
```

Now that the Bookstore object is initialized, you need to tell MasterViewController how to display the list of books—not the detail, just the book titles. To do this, you'll need to modify a few methods. Fortunately, Xcode has provided a nice template, so the modifications are small.

MasterViewController is a subclass of what's called a UITableViewController class, which displays rows of data to the screen. In this case, these are rows of book titles (well, just two for this simple program but a list nonetheless).

There are three main methods that control what and how data is displayed in a UITableViewController.

■ The first is numberOfSectionsInTableView(_:): Since the application has only one list, or section, this method returns 1.

■ The second is tableView(_:numberOfRowsInSection:): In this program, you return the number of books in the bookstore array. Since this is the only section, the code is straightforward.

■ The third method is tableView(_:cellForRowAtIndexPath:): This method is called for each row that is to be displayed on the screen, and it's called one row at a time.

Listing 8-14 details the changes you need to make to get the list of books displaying on the view. The changes start at line 83 in the source file.

Listing 8-14. Setting Up the View to Display the Books

```
83
84          override func numberOfSectionsInTableView(tableView: UITableView) -> Int {
85              return 1
86          }
87
88          override func tableView(tableView: UITableView, numberOfRowsInSection section: Int) -> Int {
89
90              return myBookStore.theBookStore.count
91          }
92
93          override func tableView(tableView: UITableView, cellForRowAtIndexPath indexPath:
            NSIndexPath) -> UITableViewCell {
94
95              let cell = tableView.dequeueReusableCellWithIdentifier("Cell", forIndexPath:
                indexPath) as UITableViewCell
96
97              cell.textLabel.text? = myBookStore.theBookStore[indexPath.row].title
98              cell.accessoryType = UITableViewCellAccessoryType.DisclosureIndicator
99              return cell
100         }
```

Out of all of this code, you need to modify only a few lines. Everything else can stay the way it is. This is one of the advantages of using the Xcode templates. Line 90 simply returns 1; you need to change it so that it now returns the count of items in the Bookstore class.

Line 97 looks a little more complicated. Basically, each line of the UITableView is what is called a *cell* (a UITableViewCell to be specific). Line 97 sets the text of the cell to the title of a book. Let's look at that code a little more specifically:

```
cell.textLabel.text = myBookStore.theBookStore[indexPath.row].title
```

First, myBookStore is the Bookstore object, which is pretty clear. You're referencing the array in the Bookstore object called theBookStore. Since theBookStore is an array, you can access the book you want in brackets in the indexPath.row. The value indexPath.row specifies which row you're interested in—indexPath.row will always be less than the total count minus 1 (returned on line 90). So, calling myBookStore.theBookStore[indexPath.row] returns a Book object. The last part, .title, accesses the title property from the returned Book object. The following code is equivalent to what you just did in one line:

```
1    var book: Book
2    book = myBookStore.theBookStore[indexPath.row]
3    cell.textLabel.text = book.title
```

Now, you should be able to build and run the application and see the two books you created in the data model, as shown in Figure 8-15.

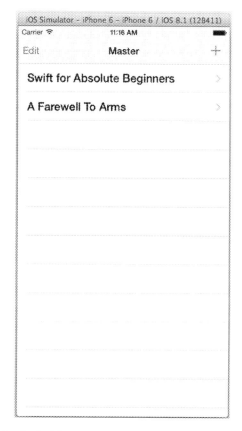

Figure 8-15. Running the application for the first time

But, you're not done yet. You need to make the application display the book when you click one of them. To make this happen, you need to make one last modification to MasterViewController.

The method tableView(_:didSelectRowAtIndexPath:) is called whenever a row is touched on the screen. Listing 8-15 shows the small changes you need to make in order to hook up the detail view with the book data.

Listing 8-15. Selecting the Book When Touched

```
146        override func prepareForSegue(segue: UIStoryboardSegue, sender: AnyObject?) {
147            if segue.identifier == "showDetail" {
148                if let indexPath = self.tableView.indexPathForSelectedRow() {
149                    let selectedBook:Book = myBookStore.theBookStore[indexPath.row]
150                    (segue.destinationViewController as DetailViewController).detailItem =
                       selectedBook
151                }
152            }
153        }
154
155
156
157
158
```

If line 149 looks similar to line 97 in Listing 8-14, that's because it's basically the same thing. Based upon indexPath.row, you select the specific book from the Bookstore object and save it in a variable called selectedBook.

On line 150, you take selectedBook and store it in a property called detailItem that is already part of the existing DetailViewController class. That's all you need to do in MasterViewController. You've basically passed off the book to DetailViewController. You're almost done. Now you need to make a few small modifications to the DetailViewController so that it displays the Book object properly.

Modifying the DetailViewController

Earlier in this chapter, you modified the DetailViewController so that it would display some detail information about a book. In the code you just finished, you modified the MasterViewController so that it passes the selected book to the DetailViewController. Now all that remains is to simply move the information from the Book object in the DetailViewController to the appropriate fields on the screen. All of this is done in one method—configureView as seen in Listing 8-16.

Listing 8-16. Moving the Book Object Data to the Detail View

```
33        func configureView() {
34            if let detail: AnyObject = self.detailItem {
35                var myBook = detail as Book
36                titleLabel.text = myBook.title
37                authorLabel.text = myBook.author
38                descriptionTextView.text = myBook.description
39            }
40
41        }
42
43
```

The configureView method is one of many convenience methods included in the Xcode template and is called whenever the DetailViewController is being initialized. This is where you will move your selected Book object's information to the fields in the view.

Lines 36 to 38 in the DetailViewController.swift file is where you move the information from the Book object to the view. If you recall, line 150 in Listing 8-15 set the selected book into a property on the DetailViewController called detailItem. Lines 34 to 35 pull that item out into a Book object called myBook.

Lines 36 to 38 simply move each of the Book object's properties to the view controls you built earlier in the chapter. That's all you need to in this class. If you build and run the project and click one of the books, you should see something like Figure 8-16.

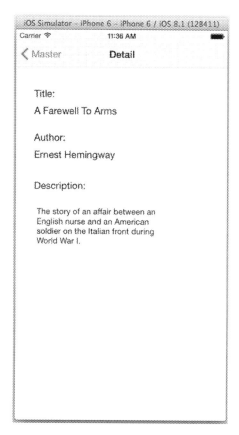

Figure 8-16. Viewing the book details for the first time

Summary

You've reached the end of this chapter! Here is a summary of the topics covered:

- *Understanding collection classes*: Collection classes are a powerful set of classes that come with Foundation and allow you to store and retrieve information efficiently.

- *Using variables*: Instance variables are variables that are accessible once the class has been instantiated.

- *Looping with for…in: This* feature offers a new way to iterate through an enumerated list of items.

- *Building a master-detail application*: You used Xcode and the Master-Detail Application template to build a simple bookstore program to display books and the details of an individual book.

▓ *A simple data model*: Using the collection classes you learned about, you used an array to construct a `Bookstore` object and use it as a data source in the bookstore program.

▓ *Connect data to the view*: You connected the `Book` object's data to the interface fields using Xcode.

Exercises

▓ Add more books to the bookstore using the original program as a guide.

▓ Enhance the `Book` class so it can store another attribute—a price or ISBN, for example.

▓ Modify the `DetailViewController` so that the new fields are displayed. Remember to connect an interface control to an instance variable.

▓ Change the `Bookstore` object so that a separate method is called to initialize the list of `Book` objects (instead of putting it all in the `init` method).

▓ There is another attribute to a `UITableViewCell` called the `detailTextLabel`. Try to make use of this by setting its `text` property to something.

▓ Using Xcode to modify the interface, play with changing the background color of the `DetailViewController` in the storyboard file.

For a tougher challenge:

▓ Sort the books in the `Bookstore` object so they appear in ascending order on the `MasterDetailView`.

Chapter **9**

Comparing Data

In this chapter, I will discuss one of the most basic and frequent operations you will perform as you program: comparing data. In the bookstore example, you may need to compare book titles if your clients are looking for a specific book. You may also need to compare authors if your clients are interested in purchasing books by a specific author. Comparing data is a common task performed by developers. Many of the loops you learned about in the previous chapter will require you to compare data so that you know when your code should stop looping.

Comparing data in programming is like using a scale. You have one value on one side and another value on the other side. In the middle, you have an operator. The operator determines what kind of comparison is being done. Examples of operators are "greater than," "less than," or "equal to."

The values on either side of the scale are usually variables. You learned about the different types of variables in Chapter 3. In general, the comparison functions for different variables will be slightly different. It is imperative that you become familiar with the functions and syntax to compare data because this will form the basis of your development.

For the purposes of this chapter, I will use an example of a bookstore application. This application will allow users to log in to the application, search for books, and purchase them. I will cover the different ways of comparing data to show how they would be used in this type of application.

Revisiting Boolean Logic

In Chapter 4 I introduced Boolean logic. Because of its prevalence in programming, I will revisit this subject in this chapter and go into more detail.

The most common comparison that you will program your application to perform is comparisons using Boolean logic. Boolean logic usually comes in the form of if/then statements. Boolean logic can have only one of two answers: yes or no. The following are some good examples of Boolean questions that you will use in your applications:

- Is 5 larger than 3?
- Does *now* have more than five letters?
- Is 6/1/2010 later than today?

Notice that there are only two possible correct answers to these questions: yes and no. If you are asking a question that could have more than these two answers, that question will need to be worded differently for programming.

Each of these questions will be represented by an if/then statement (for example, "If 5 is greater than 3, then print a message to the user"). Each if statement is required to have some sort of relational operator. A relational operator can be something like "is greater than" or "is equal to."

To start using these types of questions in your programs, you will first need to become familiar with the different relational operators available to you in the Swift language. I will cover them first. After that, you will learn how different variables can behave with these operators.

Using Relational Operators

Swift uses six standard comparison operators. These are the standard algebraic operators with only one real change: in the Swift language, as in most other programming languages, the "equal to" operator is made by two equal signs (==).Table 9-1 describes the operators available to you as a developer.

Table 9-1. Comparison Operators

>	Greater than
<	Less than
>=	Greater than or equal to
<=	Less than or equal to
==	Equal to

Note   A single equal sign (=) is used to assign a value to a variable. Two equal signs (==) are needed to compare two values. For example, if(x=9) will assign the value of 9 to the variable x and return yes if 9 is successfully assigned to x, which will be in most, if not all, of the cases. if(x==9) will do a comparison to see whether x equals 9.

Comparing Numbers

One of the difficulties developers have had in the past was dealing with different data types in comparisons. Earlier in this book, I discussed the different types of variables. You may remember that 1 is an integer. If you wanted to compare an integer with a float such as 1.2, this could cause some issues. Thankfully, Swift helps with this. In Swift, you can compare any two numeric data types without having to typecast. (Typecasting is still sometimes needed when dealing with other data types, which I cover later in the chapter.) This allows you to write code without worrying about the data types that need to be compared.

> **Note**   Typecasting is the conversion of an object or variable from one type to another.

In the bookstore application, you will need to compare numbers in many ways. For example, let's say the bookstore offers a discount for people who spend more than $30 in a single transaction. You will need to add the total amount the person is spending and then compare this to $30. If the amount spent is larger than $30, you will need to calculate the discount. See the following example:

```
var discountThreshold = 30
var discountPercent = 0
var totalSpent = calculateTotalSpent()

if(totalSpent > discountThreshold) {
    discountPercent = 10
}
```

Let's walk through the code. First, you declare the variables (totalSpent, discountThreshhold, and discountPercent) and assign a value to them. Notice you do not need to specify the type of number for the variables. The type will be assigned when you assign it a value. You know that discountThreshold and discountPercent will not contain decimals, so the compiler will create them as Ints. In this example, you can assume you have a function called calculateTotalSpent, which will calculate the total spent in this current order. You then simply check to see whether the total spent is larger than the discount threshold; if it is, you set the discount percent. Also notice that it was not necessary to tell the code to convert the data when comparing the different numeric data types. As I mentioned earlier, Swift handles all this.

Another action that requires the comparison of numbers is looping. As discussed in Chapter 4, looping is a core action in development, and many loop types require some sort of comparison to determine when to stop. Let's take a look at a for loop:

```
var numberOfBooks: Int
numberOfBooks = 50

for var y = 1; y <= numberOfBooks; y++  {
    doSomething()
}
```

In this example, you iterate, or *loop*, through the total number of books in the bookstore. The `for` statement is where the interesting stuff starts to happen. Let's break it down.

The following portion of the code is declaring y as a variable and then assigning it a starting value of 1:

```
var y = 1;
```

The following portion is telling the computer to check to see whether the counting variable y is less than or equal to the total number of books you have in the store. If y becomes larger than the number of books, the loop will no longer run.

```
y <= numberOfBooks;
```

The following portion of code increases y by 1 every time the loop is run.

```
y++
```

Creating an Example Xcode App

Now let's create an Xcode application so you can start comparing numeric data.

1. Launch Xcode. From the Finder, go to the Applications folder. Drag it to the Dock because you will be using it throughout the rest of this book. See Figure 9-1.

Figure 9-1. Launching Xcode

2. Click "Create a new Xcode project" to open a new window. On the left side of that window, under iOS, select Application. Then select Single View Application on the right side. Click Next, as shown in Figure 9-2.

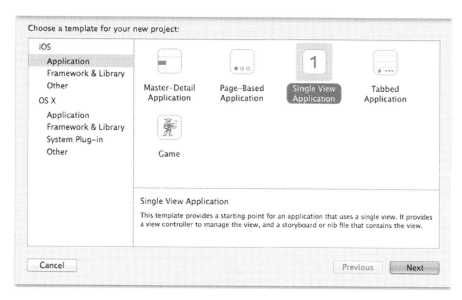

Figure 9-2. Creating a new project

> **Note**   The Single View Application template is the most generic and basic of the iOS application types.

3. On the next page, enter the name of your application. Here I used **Comparison** as the name, but you can choose any name you like. This is also the window where you select which device you would like to target. Leave it as iPhone for now, as shown in Figure 9-3.

Figure 9-3. Selecting the project type and name

> **Note**   Xcode projects, by default, are saved in the Documents folder in your user home.

4. Once the new project is created, you will see the standard Xcode window. Select the arrow next to the Comparison folder to expand it. You will see several files. The main file for your project is the AppDelegate.swift file. You will also see a ViewController.swift file. This file is the source that controls the single window that is created by default for you in this type of app. For the purposes of these examples, you will be focusing on the AppDelegate.swift file.

5. Click the AppDelegate.swift file, and you will see the following code:

```
func application(application: UIApplication, didFinishLaunchingWithOptions launchOptions:
[NSObject: AnyObject]?) -> Bool {
        // Override point for customization after application launch.
        return true
    }
```

6. The method application: didFinishLaunchingWithOptions is called after each time the application is launched. At this point, your application will just launch and display a window. You will add a little Hello World to your application. Before the line return true, you need to add the following code:

```
NSLog("Hello World")
```

This line creates a new String with the contents Hello World and passes it to the NSLog function that is used for debugging.

> **Note**   The NSLog method is available to Objective-C and Swift. It is commonly used for debugging an application because you can show information easily in the Debug area.

Let's run the application to see how it works:

1. Click the Run button in the default toolbar.

2. The iOS simulator will launch. This will just display a window. Back in Xcode, a Console window will appear at the bottom of the screen, as shown in Figure 9-4. You can always toggle this window by selecting View ➤ Debug Area ➤ Show / Hide Debug Area.

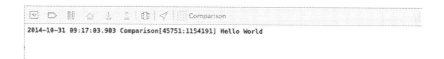

Figure 9-4. *Debugger window*

You will now see a line of text in your debugger. The first part of the line shows the date, time, and name of the application. The Hello World part was generated by the NSLog line that you added.

1. Go back to Xcode and open the AppDelegate.swift file.

2. Go to the beginning of the line that begins with NSLog. This is the line that is responsible for printing the Hello World section. You are going to comment out this line by placing two forward slashes (//) in front of the line of code. Commenting out code tells Xcode to ignore it when it builds and runs the application. In other words, code that is commented out will not run.

3. Once you comment out the line of code, you will no longer see the line in bold if you run the program because the application is no longer outputting any line.

4. For the application to output the results of your comparisons, you will have to add one line, as shown here:

```
NSLog("The result is %@", (6 > 5 ? "True" : "False"))
```

> **Note**   The previous code, (6>5 ? "True" : "False"), is called a *ternary* operation. It is essentially just a simplified way of writing an if/then statement.

5. Place this line in your code. This line is telling your application to print The
    result is. Then it will print True if 6 is greater than 5, or it will print False if 5
    is greater than 6.

Because 6 is greater than 5, it will print True.

You can change this line to test any of the examples you have put together thus far in this chapter or
any of the examples you will do later.

Let's try another example.

```
var i = 5
var y = 6
NSLog("The result is %@", (y > i ? "True" : "False"))
```

In this example, you create an variable and assign its value to 5. You then create another variable and
assign the value to 6. You then change the NSLog example to compare the variables i and y instead of
using actual numbers. When you run this example, you will get the result shown in Figure 9-5.

```
2014-12-08 07:38:03.694 Comparison[19504:431766] The result is True
```

Figure 9-5. NSLog output

> **Note**   You may get compiler warnings when using this code. The compiler will tell you that the false portion
> of the ternary operator will never be executed. The compiler can look at the values while you are typing the
> code and know that the comparison will be true.

You will now explore other kinds of comparisons, and then you will come back to the application and
test some of them.

Using Boolean Expressions

A Boolean expression is the easiest of all comparisons. Boolean expressions are used to determine
whether a value is true or false. Here's an example:

```
var j = 5
if  j > 0 {
    some_code()
}
```

The if statement will always evaluate to true because the variable j is greater than zero. Because of
that, the program will run the some_code() method.

If you change the value of `j`, the statement will evaluate to `false` because `j` is now 0. This can be used with `Bool` and number variables.

```
var j = 0
if j > 0 {
    some_code()
}
```

Placing an exclamation point in front of a Boolean expression will change it to the opposite value (a `false` becomes a `true`, and a `true` becomes a `false`). This line now asks "If not j>0," which, in this case, is `true` because `j` is equal to zero. This is an example of using an integer to act as a Boolean variable. As I discussed earlier, Swift also has variables called `Bool` that have only two possible values: `true` or `false`.

```
var j = 0
if !(j > 0) {
    some_code()
}
```

Let's look at an example related to the bookstore. Say you have a frequent buyers' club that entitles all members to a 15 percent discount on all books they purchase. This is easy to check. You simply set the variable `clubMember` to `true` if they are a member and no if they are not. The following code will apply the discount only to club members:

```
var discountPercent = 0
var clubMember: Bool = false

if(clubMember) {
    discountPercent = 15
        }
```

Comparing Strings

Strings are a difficult data type for most C languages. In ANSI C (or standard C), a string is just an array of characters. Objective-C took the development of the string even further and made it an object called NSString. Swift has taken the String class even further and made it easier to work with. Many more properties and methods are available to you when working with an object. Fortunately for you, String has many methods for comparing data, which makes your job much easier.

Let's look at an example. Here, you are comparing passwords to see whether you should allow a user to log in:

```
var enteredPassword = "Duck"
var myPassword = "duck"

var continueLogin = false

if enteredPassword == myPassword {
    continueLogin = true
}
```

The first line just declares a String and sets it value to Duck. The next line declares another string and sets its value to duck. In your actual code, you will need to get the enteredPassword string from the user.

The next line is the part of the code that actually does the work. You simply ask the strings if they are equal to each other. The example code will always be false because of the capital on the enteredPassword versus the lowercase on the myPassword.

There are many other different comparisons you might have to perform on strings. For example, you may want to check the length of a certain string. This is easily done.

```
var enteredPassword = "Duck"
var myPassword = "duck"
var continueLogin = false
if countElements(enteredPassword) > 5 {
    continueLogin = true
 }
```

> **Note**   countElements is a global function that can be used to count strings, arrays, and dictionaries.

This code checks to see whether the entered password is longer than five characters.

There will be other times when you will have to search within a string for some data. Fortunately, Swift makes this easy to do. String provides a function called rangeOfString, which allows you to search within a string for another string. The function rangeOfString takes only one argument, which is the string for which you are searching.

```
var searchTitle: String
var bookTitle: String
searchTitle = "Sea"
bookTitle = "2000 Leagues Under the Sea"

if bookTitle.rangeOfString(searchTitle) != nil {
    addToResults()
}
```

This code is similar to other examples you have examined. This example takes a search term and checks to see whether the book title has that same search term in it. If it does, it adds the book to the results. This can be adapted to allow users to search for specific terms in book titles, authors, or even descriptions.

For a complete listing of the methods supported by String, see the Apple documentation at https://developer.apple.com/LIBRARY/PRERELEASE/IOS/documentation/General/Reference/SwiftStandardLibraryReference/index.html.

Using the switch Statement

Up to this point, you've seen several examples of comparing data by simply using the if statement or the if/else statements.

```
if (some_value == SOME_CONSTANT) {
    ...
} else if (some_value == SOME_OTHER_CONSTANT) {
    ...
} else if (some_value == YET_SOME_OTHER_CONSTANT) {
    ...
}
```

If you need to compare a variable to several constant values, you can use a different method that can simplify the comparison code: the switch statement.

> **Note**   In Objective-C, you could only use integers to compare in a switch statement. Swift allows developers more freedom in using the switch statement.

The switch statement allows the comparison of one or more values in an original variable.

```
var customerType = "Repeat"

switch  customerType {        // The switch statement followed by a begin brace
case "Repeat":                // Equivalent to if (customerType == "Repeat")
    ...                       // Call functions and put any other statements here after the case.
    ...
case "New":
    ...
    ...
```

```
case "Seasonal":                    ...
   ...
default:                  // Default is required in Swift

}  // End of the switch statement.
```

The `switch` statement is powerful, and it simplifies and streamlines comparisons of a Boolean operator to several different values.

In Swift, the `switch` statement is a powerful statement that can be used to simplify repeated `if/else` statements.

Comparing Dates

Dates are a fairly complicated variable type in any language, and unfortunately, depending on the type of application you are writing, they are common. Swift does not have its own native `Date` type. This means developers will have to use the Cocoa date type `NSDate`. The `NSDate` class has a lot of nice methods that make comparing dates easy. I will focus on the `compare` function. The `compare` function returns an `NSComparisonResult`, which has three possible values: `OrderedSame`, `OrderedDescending`, and `OrderedAscending`.

```
// Today's Date
var today: NSDate = NSDate()

// Sale Date = Tomorrow
let timeToAdd: NSTimeInterval = 60*60*24
var saleDate: NSDate = today.dateByAddingTimeInterval(timeToAdd)

var saleStarted = false
let result: NSComparisonResult  = today.compare(saleDate)

switch result {
case NSComparisonResult.OrderedAscending:
    // Sale Date is in the future
    saleStarted = false
case NSComparisonResult.OrderedDescending:
    // Sale Start Date is in the past so sale is on
    saleStarted = true
default:
    // Sale Start Date is now
    saleStarted = true
}
```

This may seem like a lot of work just to compare some dates. Let's walk through the code and see whether you can make sense of it.

```
var today: NSDate = NSDate()
let timeToAdd: NSTimeInterval = 60*60*24
var saleDate: NSDate = today.dateByAddingTimeInterval(timeToAdd)
```

Here, you declare two different NSDate objects. The first one, named today, is initialized with the system date or your device date. Before creating the second date, you need to add some time to the first date. You do this by creating an NSTimeInterval. This is a number in seconds. To add a day, you add 60*60*24. The second date, named saleDate, is initialized with a date some time in the future. You will use this date to see whether this sale has begun. I will not go into detail about the initialization of NSDate objects.

> **Note**   In most programming languages, dates are dealt with in a specific pattern. They usually start with the four-digit year followed by a hyphen, then a two-digit month followed by a hyphen, and then a two-digit day. If you are using a data format with a time, this data is usually presented in a similar manner. Times are usually presented with the hour, minute, and second, each separated by a colon. Swift inherits time zone support from Cocoa. The -0700 tells Swift that the time is seven hours less than Greenwich mean time or Mountain standard time.

The results of using the compare function of an NSDate object is an NSComparisonResult. You have to declare an NSComparisonResult to capture the output from the compare function.

```
let result: NSComparisonResult = today.compare(saleDate)
```

This simple line runs the comparison of the two dates. It places the resulting NSComparisonResult into the variable called result.

```
switch result {
case NSComparisonResult.OrderedAscending:
    // Sale Date is in the future
    saleStarted = false
case NSComparisonResult.OrderedDescending:
    // Sale Start Date is in the past so sale is on
    saleStarted = true
default:
    // Sale Start Date is now
    saleStarted = true
}
```

Now you need to find out what value is in the variable result. To accomplish this, you perform a switch statement that compares the result to the three different options for NSComparisonResult. The first line finds out whether the sale date is greater than today's date. This means that the sale date is in the future, and thus the sale has not started. You then set the variable saleStarted to false. The next line finds out whether the sale date is less than today. If it is, then the sale has started, and you set the saleStarted variable to true. The next line just says default. This captures all other options. You know, though, that the only other option is OrderedSame. This means the two dates are the same, and thus the sale is just beginning.

There are other methods that you can use to compare NSDate objects. Each of these methods will be more efficient at certain tasks. I have chosen the compare method because it will handle most of your basic date comparison needs.

> **Note**   Remember that an NSDate holds both a date and a time. This can affect your comparisons with dates because it compares not only the date but the time.

Combining Comparisons

As I discussed in Chapter 4, sometimes something more complex than a single comparison is needed. This is where logical operators come in. Logical operators enable you to check for more than one requirement. For example, if you have a special discount for people who are members of your book club *and* who spend more than $30, you can write one statement to check this.

```
var totalSpent = 31
var discountThreshhold = 30
var discountPercent = 0
var clubMember = true

if totalSpent > discountThreshhold && clubMember {
    discountPercent = 15
}
```

I have combined two of the examples shown earlier. The new comparison line reads as follows: "If totalSpent is greater than discountThreshold AND clubMember is true, then set the discountPercent to 15." For this to return true, both items need to be true. You can use || instead of && to signify "or." You can change the previous line to this:

```
if totalSpent > discountThreshhold || clubMember  {
        discountPercent = 15
}
```

Now this reads as follows: "If totalSpent is greater than discountThreshold *or* clubMember is true, then set the discount percent." This will return true if either of the options is true.

You can continue to use the logical operations to string as many comparisons together as you need. In some cases, you may need to group comparisons using parentheses. This can be more complicated and is beyond the scope of this book.

Summary

You've reached the end of the chapter! Here is a summary of the topics that were covered:

- Comparisons

  - Comparing data is an integral part of any application.

- Relational operators

  - You learned about the six standard relational operators and how each is used.

- Numbers

  - Numbers are the easiest pieces of information to compare. You learned how to compare numbers in your programs.

- Example

  - You created a sample application where you could test your comparisons and make sure that you are correct in your logic.

  - You learned how to change the application to add different types of comparisons.

- Boolean

  - You learned how to check Boolean values.

- Strings

  - You learned how strings behave differently from other pieces of information you have tested.

- Dates

  - You learned how difficult it can be to compare dates and that you must be careful to make sure you are getting the response you desire.

Exercises

- Modify the example application to compare some string information. This can be in the form of either a variable or a constant.

- Write a Swift app that determines whether the following years are leap years: 1800, 1801, 1899, 1900, 2000, 2001, 2003, and 2010. Output should be written to the console in the following format: `The year 2000 is a leap year` or `The year 2001 is not a leap year`. See `http://en.wikipedia.org/wiki/Leap_year` for information on determining whether a year is a leap year.

Chapter 10

Creating User Interfaces

Interface Builder enables iOS developers to easily create their user interfaces using a powerful graphical user interface. It provides the ability to build user interfaces by simply dragging objects from Interface Builder's library to the editor.

Interface Builder stores your user interface design in one or more resource files, called storyboards and XIBs. These resource files contain the interface objects, their properties, and their relationships.

To build a user interface, simply drag objects from Interface Builder's Object Library pane onto your view or scene. Actions and outlets are two key components of Interface Builder that help you streamline the development process.

Your objects trigger actions in your views, and the actions are connected to your methods in the app's code. Outlets are declared in your `.swift` file and are connected to specific controls as properties. See Figure 10-1.

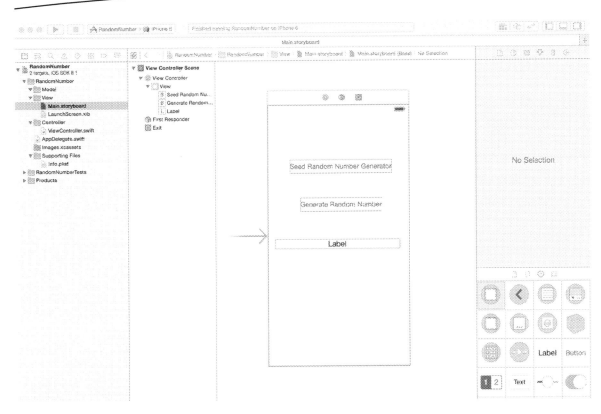

Figure 10-1. Interface Builder

> **Note**   Interface Builder was once a stand-alone application that developers used to design their user interfaces. Starting with Xcode 4.0, Interface Builder is integrated into Xcode.

Understanding Interface Builder

Interface Builder saves the user interface file as a bundle that contains the interface objects and relationships used in the application. These bundles previously had the file extension .nib. Version 3.0 of Interface Builder used a new XML file format, and the file extension changed to .xib. However, developers still call these files *nib* files. Later Apple introduced storyboards. Storyboards enable you to have all of your views in one file with a .storyboard extension.

Unlike most other graphical user interface applications, XIBs and storyboards are often referred to as *freeze-dried* because they contain the archived objects themselves and are ready to run.

The XML file format is used to facilitate storage with source control systems such as Subversion and Git.

In the next section, I'll discuss an app design pattern called Model-View-Controller. This design pattern enables developers to more easily maintain code and reuse objects over the life of an app.

The Model-View-Controller Pattern

Model-View-Controller (MVC) is the most prevalent design pattern used in iOS development, and learning about it will make your life as a developer much easier. MVC is used in software development and is considered an architectural pattern.

Architectural patterns describe solutions to software design problems that developers can use in their code. The MVC pattern is not unique to iOS developers; it is being adopted by many makers of integrated development environments (IDEs), including those running on Windows and Linux platforms.

Software development is considered an expensive and risky venture for businesses. Frequently, apps take longer than expected to write, come in over budget, and don't work as promised. Object-oriented programming (OOP) produced a lot of hype and gave the impression that companies would realize savings if they adopted its methodology, primarily because of the reusability of objects and easier maintainability of the code. Initially, this didn't happen.

When engineers looked at why OOP wasn't living up to these expectations, they discovered a key shortcoming with how developers were designing their objects: developers were frequently mixing objects in such a way that the code became difficult to maintain as the application matured, the code moved to different platforms, or hardware displays changed.

Objects were often designed so that if any of the following changed, it was difficult to isolate the objects that were impacted:

- Business rules
- User interfaces
- Client-server or Internet-based communication

Objects can be broken down into three task-related categories. It is the responsibility of the developer to ensure that each of these categories keeps their objects from drifting across other categories.

As objects are categorized in these groups, apps can be developed and maintained more easily over time. The following are examples of objects and their associated MVC category for an iPhone banking application:

Model

- Account balances
- User encryption
- Account transfers
- Account login

View

- Account balances table cell
- Account login spinner control

Controller

- ▓ Account balance view controller

- ▓ Account transfer view controller

- ▓ Logon view controller

The easiest way to remember and classify your objects in the MVC design pattern is the following:

- ▓ *Model*: Unique business or application rules or code that represent the real world

- ▓ *View*: Unique user interface code

- ▓ *Controller*: Anything that controls or communicates with the model or view objects

Figure 10-2 represents the MVC paradigm.

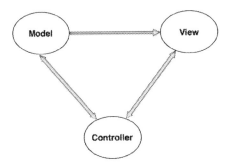

Figure 10-2. MVC paradigm

Neither Xcode nor Interface Builder forces developers to use the MVC design pattern. It is up to the developer to organize their objects in such a way to use this design pattern.

It is worth mentioning that Apple strongly embraces the MVC design pattern, and all of the frameworks are designed to work in an MVC world. This means that if you also embrace the MVC design pattern, working with Apple's classes will be much easier. If you don't, you'll be swimming upstream.

Human Interface Guidelines

Before you get too excited and begin designing dynamic user interfaces for your app, you need to learn some of the ground rules. Apple has developed one of the most advanced operating systems in the world with iOS 8. Additionally, Apple's products are known for being intuitive and user-friendly. Apple wants users to have the same experience from one app to the next.

To ensure a consistent user experience, Apple provides developers with guidelines on how their apps should look and feel. These guidelines, called the Human Interface Guidelines (HIGs), are available for the Mac, iPhone, and iPad. You can download these documents at http://developer.apple.com, as shown in Figure 10-3.

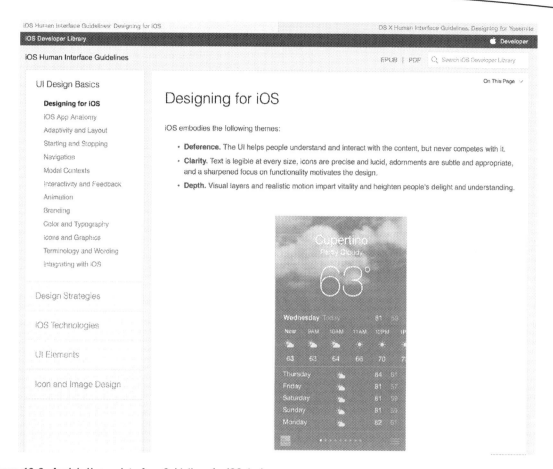

Figure 10-3. *Apple's Human Interface Guidelines for iOS devices*

Note   Apple's HIGs are more than recommendations or suggestions. Apple takes them seriously. While the HIGs don't describe how to implement your user interface designs in code, they are great for understanding the proper way to implement your views and controls.

The following are some of the top reasons apps are rejected in Apple's iTunes App Store:

- The app crashes.
- The app violates the HIGs.
- The app uses Apple's private APIs.
- The app doesn't function as advertised on iTunes App Store.

> **Note**   You can read, learn, and follow the HIGs before you develop your app, or you can read, learn, and follow the HIGs after your app gets rejected by Apple and you have to rewrite part or all of it. Either way, all iOS developers will end up becoming familiar with the HIGs.

Many new iOS developers find this out the hard way, but if you the follow the HIGs from day one, your iOS development will be a far more pleasurable experience.

Creating an Example iPhone App with Interface Builder

Let's get started by building an iPhone app that generates and displays a random number, as shown in Figure 10-4. This app will be similar to the app you created in Chapter 4, but you'll see how much more interesting the app becomes with an iOS user interface (UI).

Figure 10-4. Completed iOS random number generator app

1. Open Xcode, and select "Create a New Project". Make sure you select Single View Application for iOS; then click "Next", as shown in Figure 10-5.

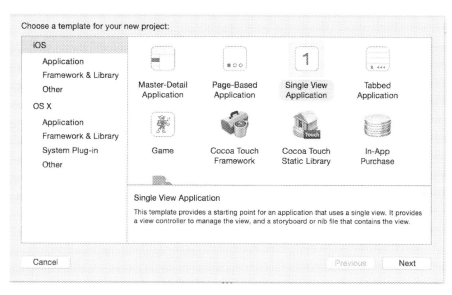

Figure 10-5. *Creating an iPhone app based on the Single View Application template*

2. Name your project **RandomNumber**, select **"Swift"** for the language and iPhone for the Device, click "Next", and save your project, as shown in Figure 10-6.

Figure 10-6. *Naming your iPhone project*

3. Your project files and settings are created and displayed, as shown in Figure 10-7.

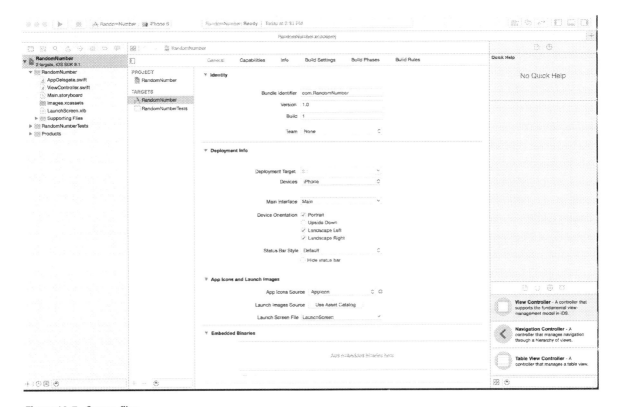

Figure 10-7. *Source files*

Although you have only one controller in this project, it's good programming practice to make your MVC groups at the beginning of your development. This helps remind you to keep the MVC paradigm and not put all of your code unnecessarily in your controller.

4. Right-click the RandomNumber project, and then select New Group, as shown in Figure 10-8.

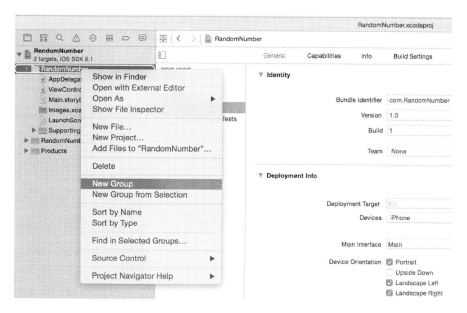

Figure 10-8. Creating new groups

5. Create a Models group, Views group, and Controllers group.

6. Drag the ViewController.swift to the Controllers group. Drag the Main.storyboard and LaunchScreen.xib files to the View group. Having these groups reminds you to follow the MVC design pattern as you develop your code and prevents you from placing all of your code in the controllers, as shown in Figure 10-9.

Figure 10-9. MVC groups with controller and storyboard files organized

Developers have found it helpful to keep their XIB files with their controllers as their projects grow. It is not uncommon to have dozens of controllers and XIB files in your project. Keeping them together helps keep everything organized. Using storyboards resolves many of the issues of having lots of XIBs.

7.   Click the `Main.storyboard` file to open Interface Builder.

Using Interface Builder

The most common way to launch Interface Builder and begin working on your view is to click the storyboard or XIB file related to the view, as shown in Figure 10-10.

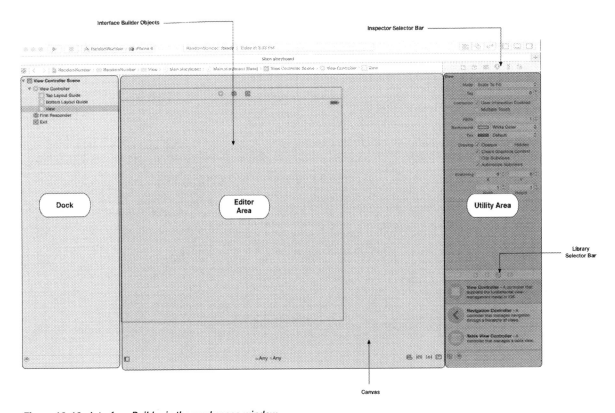

Figure 10-10. *Interface Builder in the workspace window*

When Interface Builder opens, you can see your scenes displayed on the canvas. You are now able to design your user interface. First you need to understand some of the subwindows within Interface Builder.

The Document Outline

The storyboard shows all the objects that your view contains. The following are some examples of these objects:

- Buttons
- Labels
- Text fields
- Web views
- Map views
- iAd banner views
- Picker views
- Table views

Note You can expand the width of the Document Outline to see a detailed list of all your objects, as shown in Figure 10-11. To get more real estate for the canvas, you can shrink or hide your file navigator.

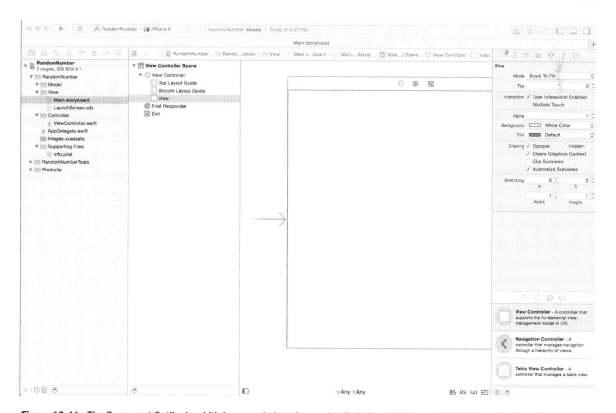

Figure 10-11. The Document Outline's width is expanded to show a detailed view of all the objects in your storyboard

The Library

The Library is where you can exploit your creativity. It's a smorgasbord of objects that you can drag and drop into the View.

- The Library pane can grow and shrink by moving the window splitter in the middle of the view, as shown in Figure 10-12.

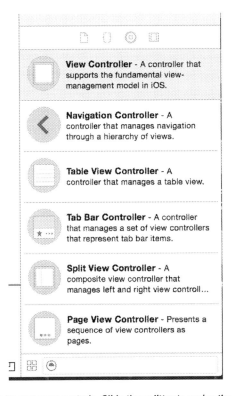

Figure 10-12. Expand the Library pane to see more controls. Slide the splitter to resize the window with the mouse

For Cocoa Touch objects, the Library contains the following (see Figure 10-13):

- Controls
- Data views
- Gesture recognizers
- Objects and controllers
- Window and bars

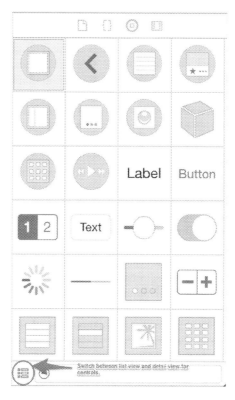

Figure 10-13. Various Cocoa Touch objects in the Library pane

Inspector Pane and Selector Bar

The Inspector pane enables you to change the properties of the controls to make your objects follow your command. The Inspector pane has six tabs across the top, as shown in Figure 10-14.

- File inspector
- Quick help inspector
- Identity inspector
- Attributes inspector
- Size inspector
- Connections inspector

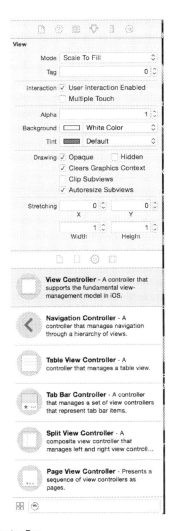

Figure 10-14. The Identity Inspector and Selector Bar

Creating the View

The random number generator will have three objects in the view: one Label and two Buttons. One Button will generate the seed, another Button will generate the random number, and the Label shows the random number generated by the app.

1. Drag a Label from the Library Pane Controls section to the View window.

2. Drag two Buttons from the Library window to the View window.

3. Click the top Button and label it **Seed Random Number Generator**.

4. Click the bottom Button and label it **Generate Random Number**, as shown in Figure 10-15.

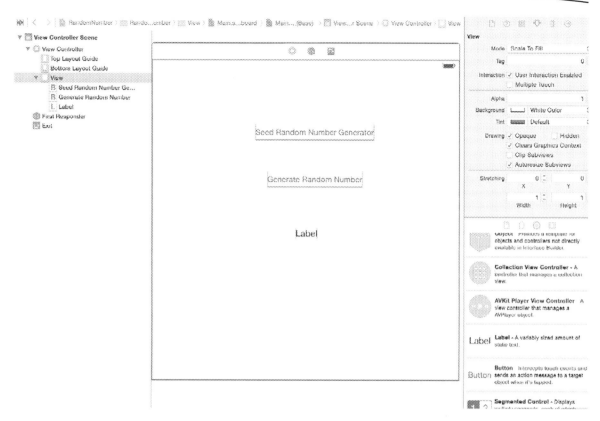

Figure 10-15. *Placing objects in the view*

Now you get to use a great feature of Xcode. You now have the ability to quickly and easily connect your outlets and actions to your code. Xcode actually goes one step further; it will create some of the code for you. All you have to do is drag and drop.

5. Click the Assistant Editor icon at the top right of the screen. This will display the associated .swift file for the view selected in the storyboard or XIB file, as shown in Figure 10-16.

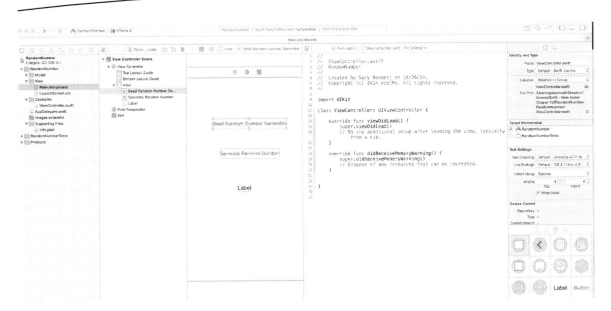

Figure 10-16. *Using the Assistant editor to display the .swift file*

> **Note**   If the correct associated `.swift` file doesn't appear when you click the Assistant Editor icon, make sure you selected and highlighted the view.

Using Outlets

Now you can connect your Label to your code by creating an outlet.

1.   Control-drag from the Label in the view to the top of your class file, as shown in Figure 10-17.

Figure 10-17. *Control-dragging to create the code for randomNumber outlet*

A pop-up window will appear. This enables you to name and specify the type of outlet.

2. Complete the pop-up as in Figure 10-18 and click the Connect button.

Figure 10-18. *Pop-up for randomNumber outlet*

The code is created for the outlet, and the outlet is now connected to the Label object in your Main.storyboard file. The shaded circle next to line 13 indicates the outlet is connected to an object in the Main.storyboard file, as shown in Figure 10-19.

```
2  //  ViewController.swift
3  //  RandomNumber
4  //
5  //  Created by Gary Bennett on 10/26/14.
6  //  Copyright (c) 2014 xcelMe. All rights reserved.
7  //
8
9  import UIKit
10
11 class ViewController: UIViewController {
12
13     @IBOutlet var randomNumber: UILabel!
14
15     override func viewDidLoad() {
16         super.viewDidLoad()
17         // Do any additional setup after loading the view, typically
               from a nib.
18     }
19
20     override func didReceiveMemoryWarning() {
21         super.didReceiveMemoryWarning()
22         // Dispose of any resources that can be recreated.
23     }
24
```

Figure 10-19. *Outlet property code generated and connected to the Label object*

There is a declaration that may be new to you called IBOutlet, commonly referred to simply as an *outlet*. Outlets signal to your controller that this property is connected to an object in Interface Builder. IBOutlet will enable Interface Builder to see the outlet and enable you to connect the property to the object in Interface Builder.

Using the analogy of an electrical wall outlet, these property outlets are connected to objects. Using Interface Builder, you can connect these properties to the appropriate object. When you change the properties of a connected outlet, the object that it is connected to will automatically change.

Using Actions

User interface object events, also known as *actions*, trigger methods.

Now you need to connect the object actions to the buttons.

1. Control-drag from the Seed Random Number Generator button to the bottom of your class. Complete the pop-up as indicated in Figure 10-20 and click the Connect button. Make sure you change the connection to an action and not an outlet.

Figure 10-20. Completing the pop-up for the Seed method

2. Repeat step 8 for the Generate Random Number button (see Figure 10-21).

Figure 10-21. *Generate and Seed actions connected to their Button objects*

The Class

All that is left is to complete the code for your outlet and actions in the .swift file for the controller.

Open the ViewController.swift file and complete the seed and generate methods, as shown in Figure 10-22.

Figure 10-22. *The seed and generate methods completed*

There is some code you should examine a bit further. The following line seeds the random generator so that you get a more random number each time you run the app. There are easier ways of to do this, but for the purposes of this section, you just want to see how actions and outlets work.

```
srandom(CUnsignedInt(time(nil)))
```

In the following code, the property `text` sets the `UILabel` value in your view. The connection you established in Interface Builder from your outlet to the Label object does all the work for you.

```
randomNumber.text
```

There are just two more things you need to do now. Select `Main.storyboard` and then click Show the File Inspector in the Inspector Pane toolbar. Deselect Use Auto Layout. A message box will appear; click Disable Size Classes. This will enable you to easily view your controls on your iPhone simulator, as shown in Figure 10-23.

Figure 10-23. Disabling Auto Layout

Lastly, center your objects in the view and expand your Label object. Also, select the center alignment property for the label. This will center your text in the Label object, as shown in Figure 10-24.

Figure 10-24. Centering your objects

That's it!

To run your iPhone app in the iPhone simulator, click the Play button, and your app should launch in the simulator, as shown in Figure 10-25.

iOS Simulator - iPhone 5 - iPhone 5 / iOS 8.1 (...

Carrier 📶   9:45 PM   ▬

Seed Random Number Generator

Generate Random Number

67

Figure 10-25. *The completed random number generator app running in the iOS simulator*

To seed the random function, tap Seed Random Number Generator. To generate the random number, tap Generate Random Number.

Summary

Great job! Interface Builder saves you a lot of time when creating user interfaces. You have a powerful set of objects to use in your application and are responsible for a minimal amount of coding. Interface Builder handles many of the details you would normally have to deal with.

You should be familiar with the following terms:

- Storyboard and XIB files
- Model-View-Controller
- Architectural patterns
- Human Interface Guidelines
- Outlets
- Actions

Exercises

- Extend the random number generator app to show a date and time in a Label when the app starts.
- After showing a date and time label, add a button to update the data and time label with the new time.

Chapter

11

Chapter

Storing Information

As a developer, there will be many different situations in which you will need to store data. Users will expect your application (*app*) to remember preferences and other information each time they launch it. Previous chapters discussed the BookStore app. With this app, users will expect your application to remember all of the books in the bookstore. Your application will need a way to store this information, retrieve it, and possibly search and sort this data. Working with data can sometimes be difficult. Fortunately, Apple has provided methods and frameworks to make this process easier.

This chapter will discuss two different formats in which data will need to be stored. It will discuss how to save preferences for the Mac and the iPhone and then discuss how to use a SQLite database in your application to store and retrieve data.

Storage Considerations

There are some major storage differences between the Mac and the iPhone, and these differences will affect how you work with data. Let's start by discussing the Mac and how you will need to develop for it.

On the Mac, by default, applications are stored in the Applications folder. Each user has their own home folder where preferences and information related to that user are stored. Not all of the users will have access to write to the Applications folder or to the application bundle itself.

On the iPhone (and iPad), developers do not need to deal with different users. Every person who uses the iPhone has the same permissions and the same folders. There are some other factors to consider with the iPhone, though. Every application on the iPhone is in its own *sandbox*. This means that files written by an application can be seen and used only by that individual application. This makes for a more secure environment for the iPhone, but it also presents some changes in the way you work with data storage.

Preferences

There are some things to consider when deciding where to store certain kinds of information. The easiest way to store information is within the preferences file, but this method has some downsides.

- All of the data is both read and written at the same time. If you are going to be writing often or writing large amounts of data, this could take time and slow down your application. As a general rule, your preferences file should never be larger than 100KB. If your preferences file starts to become larger than 100KB, consider using Core Data as a way to store your information.

- The preferences file does not provide many options when it comes to searching and ordering information.

The preferences file is really nothing more than a standardized file with accompanying classes and methods to store application-specific information. A preference would be, for example, the sorting column and direction (ascending/descending) of a list. Anything that is generally customizable within an app should be stored in a preferences file.

Writing Preferences

Apple has provided developers with the NSUserDefaults class; this class makes it easy to read and write preferences for the iPhone and Mac OS X. The great thing is that, in this case, you can use the same code for iOS and Mac OS X. The only difference between the two implementations is the location of the preferences file.

> **Note**   For Mac OS X, the preferences file is named com.yourcompany.applicationname.plist and is located in the /Users/username/Library/Preferences folder. On iOS, the preferences file is located in your application bundle in the /Library/Preferences folder.

All you need to do to write preferences is to create an NSUserDefaults object. This is done with the following line:

```
var prefs: NSUserDefaults = NSUserDefaults.standardUserDefaults()
```

This instantiates the prefs object so you can use it to set preference values. Next, you need to set the preference keys for the values that you want to save. The BookStore app example will be used to demonstrate specific instructions throughout this chapter. When running a bookstore, you might want to save a username or password in the preferences. You also might want to save things such as a default book category or recent searches. The preferences file is a great place to store this type of information because this is the kind of information that needs to be read only when the application is launched.

Also, on iOS, it is often necessary to save your current state. If a person is using your application and then gets a phone call, you want to be able to bring them back to the exact place they were in your application when they are done with their phone call. This is less necessary now with the implementation of multitasking, but your users will still appreciate it if your application remembers what they were doing the next time they launch it.

Once you have instantiated the object, you can just call setObjectforKey to set an object. If you wanted to save the username of sherlock.holmes, you would call the following line of code:

```
prefs.setObject("sherlock.holmes", forKey: "username")
```

You can use setInteger, setDouble, setBool, setFloat, and setURL instead of setObject, depending on the type of information you are storing in the preferences file. Let's say you store the number of books a user wants to see in the list. Here is an example of using setInteger to store this preference:

```
prefs.setInteger(10, forKey:"booksInList")
```

After a certain period of time, your app will automatically write changes to the preferences file. You can force your app to save the preferences by calling the synchronize function, but this is not necessary in most cases. To call the synchronize function, you would write the following line:

```
prefs.synchronize()
```

With just three lines of code, you are able to create a preference object, set two preference values, and write the preferences file. It is an easy and clean process. Here is all of the code:

```
var prefs: NSUserDefaults = NSUserDefaults.standardUserDefaults()
prefs.setObject("sherlock.holmes", forKey: "username")
prefs.setInteger(10, forKey:"booksInList")
```

Reading Preferences

Reading preferences is similar to writing preferences. Just like with writing, the first step is to obtain the NSUserDefaults object. This is done in the same way as it was done in the writing process:

```
var prefs: NSUserDefaults = NSUserDefaults.standardUserDefaults()
```

Now that you have the object, you are able to access the preference values that are set. For writing, you use the setObject syntax; for reading, you use the stringForKey method. You use the stringForKey method because the value you put in the preference was a String. In the writing example, you set preferences for the username and for the number of books in the list to display. You can read those preferences by using the following simple lines of code:

```
var username = prefs.stringForKey("username")
var booksInList = prefs.integerForKey("booksInList")
```

Pay close attention to what is happening in each of these lines. You start by declaring the variable username, which is a String. This variable will be used to store the preference value of the username you stored in the preferences. Then, you just assign it to the value of the preference username. You will notice that in the read example you do not use the `synchronize` function. This is because you have not changed the values of the preferences; therefore, you do not need to make sure they are written to a disk.

Databases

You have learned how to store some small pieces of information and retrieve them at a later point. What if you have more information that needs to be stored? What if you need to conduct a search within this information or put it in some sort of order? These kinds of situations call for a database.

A database is a tool for storing a significant amount of information in a way that it can be easily searched or retrieved. When using a database, usually small chunks of the data are retrieved at a time rather than the entire file. Many applications you use in your daily life are based on databases of some sort. Your online banking application retrieves your account activity from a database. Your supermarket uses a database to retrieve prices for different items. A simple example of a database is a spreadsheet. You may have many columns and many rows in your spreadsheet. The columns in your spreadsheet represent different types of information you want to store. In a database, these are considered *attributes*. The rows in your spreadsheet would be considered different *records* in your database.

Storing Information in a Database

Databases are usually an intimidating subject for a developer; most developers associate databases with enterprise database servers such as Microsoft SQL Server or Oracle. These applications can take time to set up and require constant management. For most developers, a database system like Oracle would be too much to handle. Luckily, Apple has included a small database engine called SQLite in iOS and OS X. This allows you to gain many of the features of complex database servers without the overhead.

SQLite will provide you with a lot of flexibility in storing information for your application. It stores the entire database in a single file. It is fast, reliable, and easy to implement in your application. The best thing about the SQLite database is that there is no need to install any software; Apple has taken care of that for you.

However, SQLite does have some limitations that, as a developer, you should be aware of.

- SQLite was designed to be used as a single-user database. You will not want to use SQLite in an environment where more than one person will be accessing the same database. This could lead to data loss or corruption.

- In the business world, databases can grow to become very large. It is not surprising for a database manager to handle databases as large as 500GB, and in some cases databases can become much larger than that. SQLite should be able to handle smaller databases without any issues, but you will begin to see performance issues if your database starts to get too large.

- SQLite lacks some of the backup and data restore features of the enterprise database solutions.

For the purposes of this chapter, you will focus on using SQLite as your database engine. If any of the mentioned limitations are present in the application you are developing, you may need to look into an enterprise database solution, which is beyond the scope of this book.

Note   SQLite (pronounced "sequel-lite") gets its name from Structured Query Language (SQL, pronounced "sequel"). SQL is the language used to enter, search, and retrieve data from a database.

Apple has worked hard to iron out a lot of the challenges of database development. As a developer, you will not need to become familiar with SQL because Apple has taken care of the direct database interaction for you through a framework called Core Data that makes interacting with the database much easier. Core Data has been adapted by Apple from a NeXT product called Enterprise Object Framework, and working with Core Data is a lot easier than interfacing directly with the SQLite database. Directly accessing a database via SQL is beyond the scope of this book.

Getting Started with Core Data

Let's start by creating a new Core Data project.

1. Open Xcode and select **File ➤ New Project**. To create an iOS Core Data project, select Application from the menu on the left. It is located underneath the iOS header. Then select Single View Application, as shown in Figure 11-1.

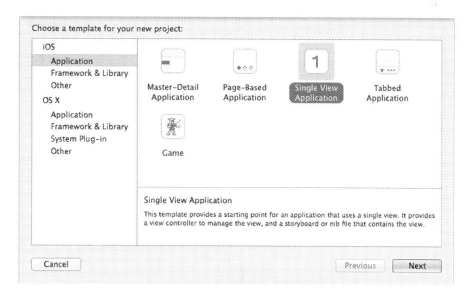

Figure 11-1. Creating a new project

2. Click the Next button when done. The next screen will allow you to enter the name you want to use. For the purposes of this chapter, you will use the name **BookStore**.

3. Near the bottom, you will see the check box Use Core Data. Make sure this is checked and then click Next, as shown in Figure 11-2.

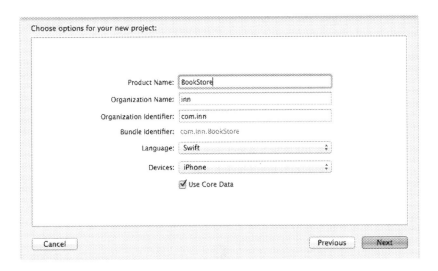

Figure 11-2. Using Core Data

Note   Core Data can be added to any project at any point. Checking that box when creating a project will add the Core Data frameworks and a default data model to your application.

4. Select a location to save the project and click Create.

Once you are done with that, your new project will open. It will look similar to a standard application, except now you will have a BookStore.xcdatamodeld file. This file is called a *data model* and will contain the information about the data that you will be storing in Core Data.

The Model

In your BookStore folder on the right, you will see a file called BookStoreCoreData.xcdatamodeld. This file will contain information about the data you want stored in the database. Click the model file to open it. You will see a window similar to the one shown in Figure 11-3.

Figure 11-3. The blank model

The window is divided into four sections. On the left you have your entities. In more common terms, these are the objects or items that you want to store in the database.

The top-right window contains the attributes. Attributes are pieces of information about the entities. For example, a book would be an entity, and the title of the book would be an attribute of that entity.

Note   In database terms, entities are your *tables*, and the attributes of the entities are called *columns*. The objects created from those entities are referred to as *rows*.

The middle window on the right will show you all the relationships of an entity. A relationship connects one entity to another. For example, you will create a Book entity and an Author entity. You will then relate them so that every book can have an author. The bottom-right portion of the screen deals with fetched properties. Fetched properties are beyond the scope of this book, but they allow you to create filters for your data.

Let's create an entity.

1. Click the plus sign in the bottom-left corner of the window, or select **Editor ➤ Add Entity** from the menu, as shown in Figure 11-4.

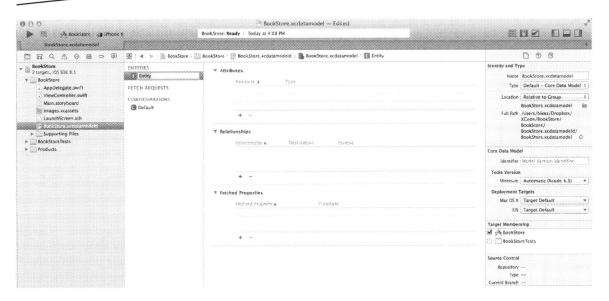

Figure 11-4. Adding a new entity

2. On the left side, name the entity Book.

> **Note**   It is required to capitalize your entities' names.

3. Now let's add some attributes. Attributes would be considered the details of a
    book, so you will store the title, author, price, and year the book was published.
    Obviously, in your own applications, you may want to store more information,
    such as the publisher, page count, and genre, but you want to start simple.
    Click the plus sign at the bottom right of the window, or select **Editor ➤
    Add Attribute**, as shown in Figure 11-5. If you do not see the option to add an
    attribute, make sure you have selected the Book entity on the left side.

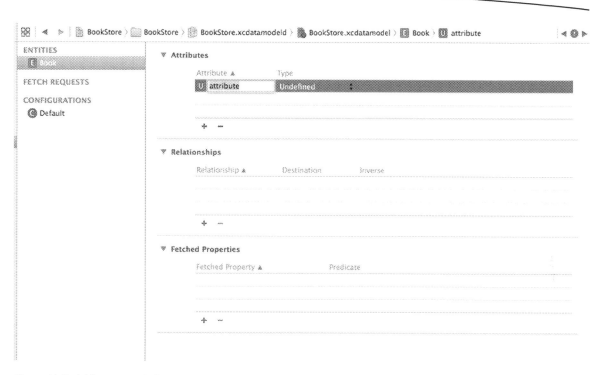

Figure 11-5. Adding a new attribute

4. You will be given only two options for your attribute, the name and the data type. Let's call this attribute `title`. Unlike entities, attribute names must be lowercase.

5. Now, you will need to select a data type. Selecting the correct data type is important. It will affect how your data is stored and retrieved from the database. The list has 12 items in it and can be daunting. We will discuss the most common options and, as you become more familiar with Core Data, you can experiment with the other options. The most common options are String, Integer 32, Decimal, and Date. For the title of the book, select String.

    String: This is the type of attribute used to store text. This should be used to store any kind of information that is not a number or a date. In this example, the book title and author will be strings.

    Integer 32: There are three different integer values possible for an attribute. Each of the integer types differ only in the minimum and maximum values possible. Integer 32 should cover most of your needs when storing an integer. An integer is a number without a decimal. If you try to save a decimal in an integer attribute, the decimal portion will be truncated. In this example, the year published will be an integer.

Decimal: A decimal is a type of attribute that can store numbers with decimals. A decimal is similar to a double attribute, but they differ in their minimum and maximum values and precision. A decimal should be able to handle any currency values. In this example, you will use a decimal to store the price of the book.

Date: A date attribute is exactly what it sounds like. It allows you to store a date and time and then performs searches and lookups based on these values. You will not use this type in this example.

6.   Let's create the rest of the attributes for the book. Now, add `price`. It should be a decimal. Add the year the book was published. For two-word attributes, it is standard to make the first word lowercase and the second word start with a capital letter. For example, an ideal name for the attribute for the year the book was published would be `yearPublished`. Select Integer 32 as the attribute type. Once you have added all of your attributes, your screen should look like Figure 11-6.

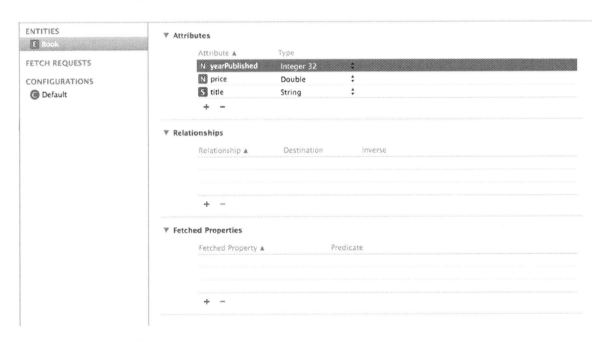

Figure 11-6. *The finished Book entity*

Note   Attribute names cannot contain spaces.

If you are used to working with databases, you will notice that you did not add a primary key. A primary key is a field (usually a number) that is used to uniquely identify each record in a database. In Core Data databases, there is no need to create primary keys. The framework will manage all of that for you.

Now that you have finished the Book entity, let's add an Author entity.

1. Add a new entity and call it Author.

2. To this entity, add lastName and firstName, both of which are considered strings.

Once this is done, you should have two entities in your relationship window. Now you need to add the relationships.

1. Click the Book entity, and then click and hold on the plus sign that is located on the bottom right of the screen. Select Add Relationship, as shown in Figure 11-7. (You can also click the plus under the Relationships section of the Core Data model.)

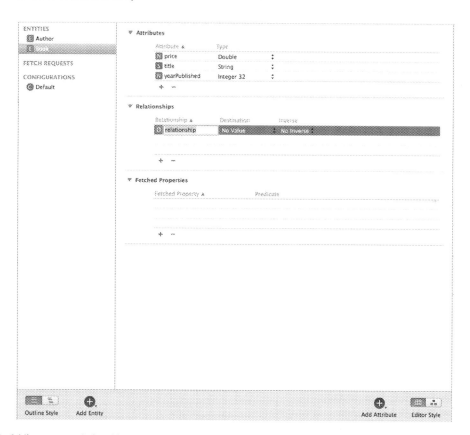

Figure 11-7. Adding a new relationship

2. You will be given the opportunity to name your relationship. You usually give a relationship the same name as the entity to which it derived from. Type in **author** as the name and select Author from the drop-down menu.

3. You have created one half of your relationship. To create the other half, click the Author entity. Click the plus sign located at the bottom right of the screen and select Add Relationship. You will use the entity name that you are connecting to as the name of this relationship, so you will call it books.

(You are adding an *s* to the relationship name because an author can have many books.) Under Destination, select Book, and under Inverse, select the relationship you made in the previous step. In the Utilities window on the right side of the screen, select the Data Model Inspector. Select To Many for the type of the relationship. Your model should now look like Figure 11-8.

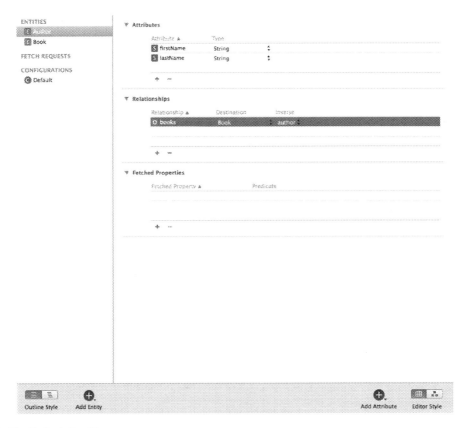

Figure 11-8. The final relationship

Note Sometimes in Xcode, when working with models, it is necessary to hit the Tab key for the names of entities, attributes, and relationships to update. This little quirk can be traced all the way back to WebObjects tools.

Now you need to tell your code about your new entity. To do this, hold down Shift and select the Book entity and the Author entity and then select **Editor ➤ Create NSManagedObject Subclass** from the Application menu. Your screen should look like Figure 11-9.

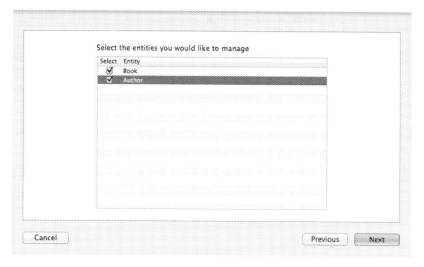

Figure 11-9. Adding the managed objects to your project

This screen allows you to select the data model you would like to create managed objects for. In this case, you have only a single data model. In some complicated applications, you may have more than one. Managed objects represent instances of an entity from your data model. Select the BookStore data model and hit Next.

You will now be presented with a screen to select the entities to create managed objects as seen in Figure 11-10. Select both and click Next.

Figure 11-10. Select the entities to create managed objects

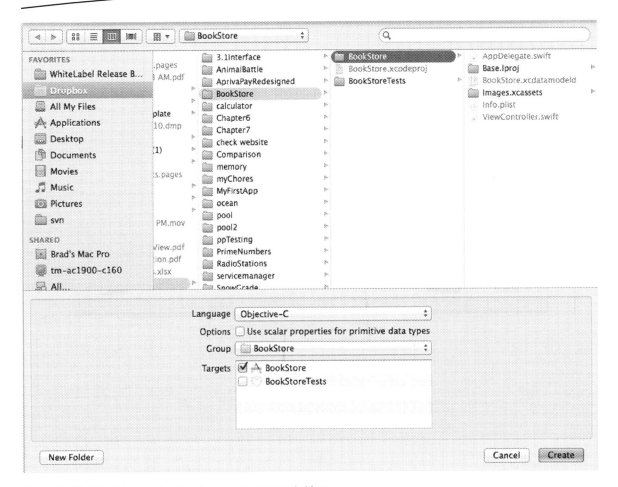

Figure 11-11. Select the save location for your new managed objects

Select the storage location and add it to your project. Make sure your language is set to Swift. By default, it is still Objective-C. You should not need to change any other defaults on this page. Then click Create. You will notice that two files have been added to your project. `Book.swift` and `Author.swift` contain the information about your books and authors. These files will need to be used to access the entities and the attributes you added to your data model. These files are fairly simple because Core Data will do most of the work with them. You should also notice that if you go back to your model and click Book, it will have a new class in the Data Model Inspector. Instead of an `NSManagedObject`, it will have a `BookStore.Book` class.

Let's look at some of the contents of `Book.swift`:

```
import Foundation
import CoreData

class Book: NSManagedObject {

    @NSManaged var title: String
    @NSManaged var price: NSDecimalNumber
    @NSManaged var yearPublished: NSNumber
    @NSManaged var author: Author

}
```

You will see that the file starts by including the Core Data framework. This allows Core Data to manage your information. In the class declaration, you will notice the superclass is `NSManagedObject`. `NSManagedObject` is an object that handles all of the Core Data database interaction. It provides the methods and properties you will be using in this example. Later in the file, you will see the three attributes and the one relationship you created.

Managed Object Context

You have created a managed object called `Book`. The nice thing with Xcode is that it will generate the necessary code to manage these new data objects. In Core Data, every managed object should exist within a managed object context. The context is responsible for tracking changes to objects, carrying out undo operations, and writing the data to the database. This is helpful because you can now save a bunch of changes at once rather than saving each individual change. This speeds up the process of saving the records. As a developer, you do not need to track when an object has been changed. The managed object context will handle all of that for you.

Setting Up the Interface

The following steps will assist you in setting up your interface:

1. In the BookStore folder in your project, you should have a `Main.storyboard` file. Click this file and Xcode will open it in the editing window, as shown in Figure 11-12.

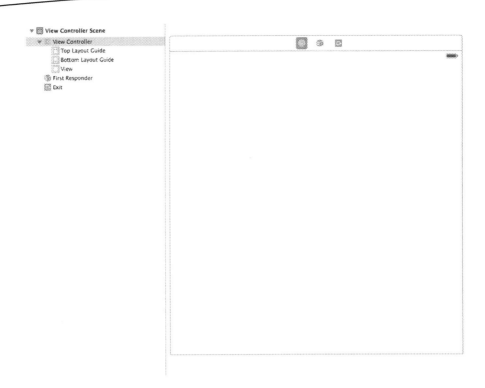

Figure 11-12. Creating the interface

2.   There should be a blank window. To add some functionality to your window, you are going to need to add some objects from the Object Library. Type **table** into the search field on the bottom right of the screen. This should narrow the objects, and you should see Table View Controller and Table View. Drag the Table View to the view, as shown in Figure 11-13.

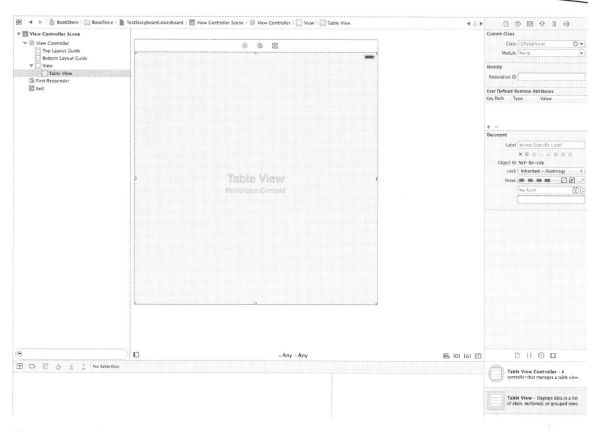

Figure 11-13. Adding the Table View

3. You now have a Table View. To create cells in your Table View, you need to
    add a UITableViewCell. Search for *cell* in your Object Library, and drag a
    Table View Cell to your table. You now have a table and a cell on your view,
    as shown in Figure 11-14.

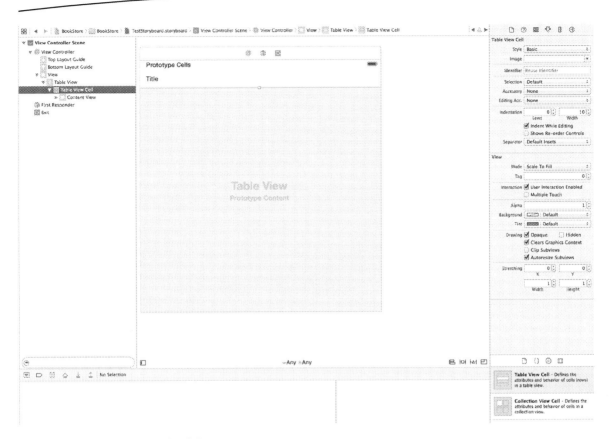

Figure 11-14. *Adding the Table View Cell*

4. Select the cell, and in the Attributes Inspector on the right side, set Style to Basic. Also, set the identifier to Cell. The identifier is used if your Table View can contain multiple types of cells. You will need to differentiate them with different identifiers. For most of your projects, you can set this to Cell and not worry about it, as shown in Figure 11-15.

Figure 11-15. *Changing the style of the cell*

5. When using a Table View, it is usually a good idea to put it in a Navigation Controller. You will be using the Navigation Controller to give you space to put an Add button on your Table View. To add a Navigation Controller, select your View Controller in the Scene box, which is the window to the left of your storyboard that shows your View Controllers (your View Controller will have a yellow icon next to it). From the Application menu, select **Editor ➤ Embed In ➤ Navigation Controller**, as shown in Figure 11-16.

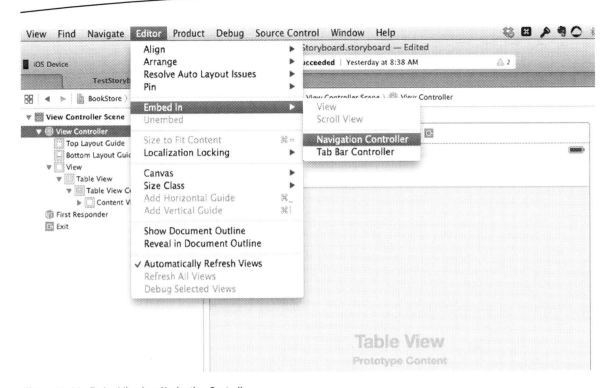

Figure 11-16. Embedding in a Navigation Controller

6. You will have a navigation bar at the top of your view. You will now add a button to the bar. This type of button is called a `UIBarButtonItem`. Search for *bar button* in your Object Library and drag a Bar Button Item to the top right of your view on the navigation bar, as shown in Figure 11-17.

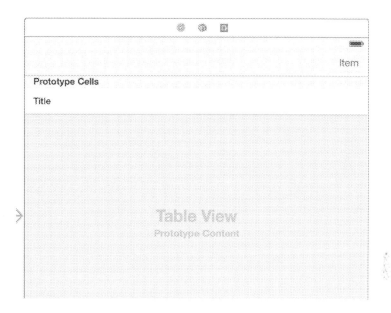

Figure 11-17. *Adding a Bar Button Item to the navigation bar*

7. Select the Bar Button Item and change Identifier to Add. This will change the look of your Bar Button Item from the word *Item* to a plus icon, as shown in Figure 11-18.

Figure 11-18. *Changing the Bar Button Item*

8. Now you have the interface created, you need to hook it up to your code. Hold down the Control key and drag your Table View to the View Controller in the Document Outline, as shown in Figure 11-19.

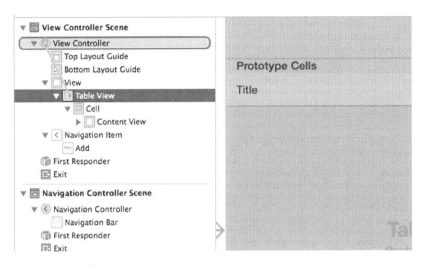

Figure 11-19. *Connecting the Table View*

9. A pop-up will appear allowing you to select either the data source or the delegate, as shown in Figure 11-20. You will need to assign both to the View Controller. The order in which you select the items does not matter, but you will have to Control-drag the Table View twice.

Figure 11-20. *Hooking up the Table View*

10. Now your Table View should be ready to go. You need to hook up your button to make it do something. In the top right of your Xcode window, click the Assistant Editor button (it looks like two circles). This will open your code on the right side and your storyboard on the left side. Now Control-drag your Add button to the View Controller code on the right, as shown in Figure 11-21.

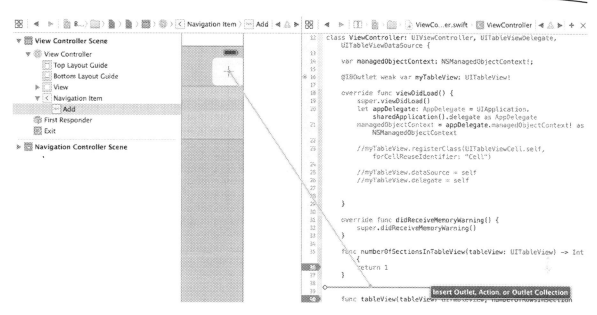

Figure 11-21. Adding an action for your Button object

11. It does not matter where you place the Add button in your code as long as it is in your class and outside of any methods. It should be after your variables just for organization. You should also place it outside your other methods. When you let go, you will be prompted for the type of connection you are creating. Set Connection to Action. Then add a name for your new method, such as **addNew**, as shown in Figure 11-22.

Figure 11-22. Changing the type and name of the connection

The interface is complete now, but you still need to add the code to make the interface do something. Go back to the Standard editor (click the list icon to the left of the two circles icon in the top right of the Xcode toolbar) and select the `ViewController.swift` file from the file list on the left side. Because you now have a Table View you have to worry about, you need to tell your class that it can handle a Table View. Change your class declaration at the top of your file to the following:

```
class ViewController: UIViewController, UITableViewDelegate, UITableViewDataSource {
```

You added `UITableViewDelegate` and `UITableViewDataSource` to your declaration. This tells your controller that it can act as a table view delegate and data source. These are called *protocols*. Protocols tell an object that they must implement certain methods to interact with other objects. For example, to conform to the `UITableViewDataSource` protocol, you need to implement the following method:

```
func tableView(tableView: UITableView, numberOfRowsInSection section: Int) -> Int
```

Without this method, the Table View will not know how many rows to draw.

Before continuing, you need to tell your `ViewController.swift` file about Core Data. To do this, you add the following line to the top of the file just under `import UIKit`:

```
import CoreData
```

You also need to add a managed object context to your `ViewController` class. Add the following line right after the `class ViewController` line:

```
var managedObjectContext: NSManagedObjectContext!;
```

Now that you have a variable to hold your `NSManagedObjectContext`, you need to instantiate it so you can add objects to it. To do this, you need to add the following lines to your `override func viewDidLoad()` method:

```
let appDelegate: AppDelegate = UIApplication.sharedApplication().delegate as AppDelegate
managedObjectContext = appDelegate.managedObjectContext! as NSManagedObjectContext
```

The first line creates a constant that points to your application delegate. The second line points your `managedObjectContext` variable to the application delegate's `managedObjectContext`. It is usually a good idea to use the same managed object context throughout your app.

The first new method you are going to add is one to query your database records. Call this method `loadBooks`.

```
1    func loadBooks() -> Array<AnyObject> {
2        var error: NSError? = nil
3        var fetchRequest = NSFetchRequest(entityName: "Book")
4        let result : [AnyObject] = managedObjectContext!.executeFetchRequest(fetchRequest,
         error:&error)!
5        return result;
6    }
```

This code is a little more complex than what you have seen before, so let's walk through it. Line 1 declares a new function called `loadBooks`, which returns an array of `AnyObject`. This means you will receive an array that can contain any type of objects you want. In this case, the objects will be `Book`. You then return the array once you have it loaded.

You will now need to add the data source methods for your Table View. These methods tell your Table View how many sections there are, how many rows are in each section, and what each cell should look like. Add the following code to your ViewController.swift file:

```
1  func numberOfSectionsInTableView(tableView: UITableView) -> Int {
2      return 1
3  }
4
5
6  func tableView(tableView: UITableView, numberOfRowsInSection section: Int) -> Int {
7      return loadBooks().count
8  }
9
10
11
12 func tableView(tableView: UITableView, cellForRowAtIndexPath indexPath: NSIndexPath) ->
   UITableViewCell {
13     var cell = tableView.dequeueReusableCellWithIdentifier("Cell") as UITableViewCell
14
15     var book: Book = loadBooks()[indexPath.row] as Book
16     cell.textLabel.text = book.title
17
18     return cell
19 }
```

In line 2, you tell your Table View that it will contain only a single section. In line 7, you call a count on your array of Book for the number of rows in your Table View. In lines 13 to 18, you create your cell and return it. Line 13 creates a cell for you to use. This is standard code for creating a cell. The identifier allows you to have more than one type of cell in a Table View, but that is more complex. Line 15 grabs your Book object from your loadBooks() array. Line 16 assigns the book title to your textLabel in the cell. The textLabel is the default label in the cell. This is all you need to do to be able to display the results of your loadBooks method in the table view. You still have one problem. You do not have any books in your database yet.

To fix this issue, you will add code to the addNew method you created earlier. Add the following code inside the addNew method you created:

```
1  @IBAction func addNew(sender: AnyObject) {
2          let entity =  NSEntityDescription.entityForName("Book", inManagedObjectContext:managedOb
           jectContext)
3
4          var book = Book(entity: entity!,insertIntoManagedObjectContext:managedObjectContext)
5
6          book.title = "My Book:" + String(loadBooks().count)
7
8          var error: NSError?
9          managedObjectContext.save(&error)
10         myTableView.reloadData()
11
12     }
```

Line 2 creates a new Book entity for your book in the database. Line 4 takes that entity and creates a Book object from it. It also inserts it into the managed object context. Remember that once it is inserted into the managed object context, its changes are tracked, and it can be saved. Line 6 sets the book title to My Book and then sets the number of items in the array. Obviously, in real life, you would want to set this to a name either given by the user or from some other list. Line 8 creates an error object just in case there is a problem saving the managed object context. Line 9 saves the managed object context. Notice that you have to pass an error object to it in case there is an issue. Line 10 tells the UITableView to reload itself to display the newly added Book. Now build and run the application. Click the + button several times. You will add new Book objects to your object store as shown in Figure 11-23. If you quit the app and relaunch it, you will notice that the data is still there.

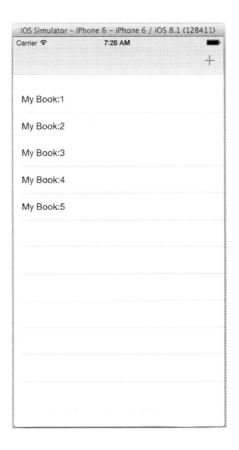

Figure 11-23. The final app

This was a cursory introduction to Core Data for iOS. Core Data is a powerful API, but it can also take a lot of time to master.

Summary

Here is a summary of the topics this chapter covered:

- Preferences

    - You learned to use `NSUserDefaults` to save and read preferences from a file, on both iOS and OS X.

- Databases

    - You learned what a database is and why using one can be preferable to saving information in a preferences file.

    - You learned about the database engine that Apple has integrated into OS X and iOS and the advantages and limitations of this database engine.

- Core Data

    - Apple provided a framework for interfacing with the SQLite database. This framework makes the interface much easier to use.

- Bookstore application

    - You created a simple Core Data application.

    - You used Xcode to create a data model for your bookstore. You learned how to create a relationship between two entities.

    - You used Xcode to create a simple interface for your Core Data model.

Exercises

- Add a new view to the app for allowing the user to enter the name of a book.

- Provide a way to remove a book from the list.

- Create an `Author` object and add it to a `Book` object.

12

Protocols and Delegates

Congratulations! You are acquiring the skills to become an iOS developer! However, iOS developers need to understand two additional topics in order to be successful: protocols and delegates. It is not uncommon for new developers to get overwhelmed by these topics, which is why we introduced the foundational topics of the Swift language first. After reading this chapter, you will see that protocols and delegates are really useful and not hard to understand and implement.

Multiple Inheritance

I discussed object inheritance in Chapter 2. In a nutshell, object inheritance means that a child can inherit all the characteristics of its parent, as shown in Figure 12-1.

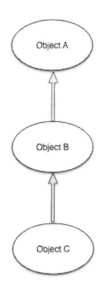

Figure 12-1. Typical Swift inheritance

C++, Perl, and Python all have a feature called *multiple inheritance*, which enables a class to inherit behaviors and features from more than one parent, as shown in Figure 12-2.

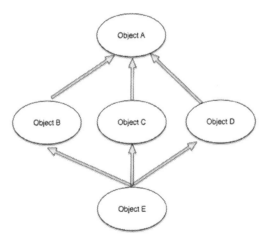

Figure 12-2. Multiple inheritance

Problems can arise with multiple inheritance because it allows for ambiguities to occur. Therefore, Swift does not implement multiple inheritances. Instead, it implements something called a *protocol*.

Understanding Protocols

Apple defines a *protocol* simply as a list of function declarations, unattached to a class definition. A protocol is similar to a class with the exception that a protocol doesn't provide an implementation for any of the requirements; it describes only what an implementation should look like.

The protocol can be adopted by a class to provide an actual implementation of those requirements. Any type that satisfies the requirements of a protocol is said to *conform* to that protocol.

Protocol Syntax

Protocols are defined like classes are, as shown in Listing 12-1.

Listing 12-1. Protocol Definition

```
protocol RandomNumberGenerator {

    var mustBeSettable: Int { get set }
    var doesNotNeedToBeSettable: Int { get }

    func random() -> Double
}
```

If a class has a superclass, you list the superclass name before any protocols it adopts, followed by a comma, as shown in Listing 12-2.

Listing 12-2. Protocol listed after super class

```
class MyClass: MySuperclass, RandomNumberGenerator, AnotherProtocol {
    // class definition goes here
}
```

The protocol also specifies whether each property must have a gettable or must have a gettable *and* settable. A gettable property is read-only, whereas a gettable and settable property is not (shown earlier in Listing 12-1).

Properties are always declared as variable properties, prefixed with var. Gettable and settable properties are indicated by { get set } after their type declaration, and gettable properties are indicated by { get }.

Delegation

Delegation is a design pattern that enables a class or structure to hand off (or *delegate*) some of its responsibilities to an instance of another type. This design pattern is implemented by defining a protocol that encapsulates the delegated responsibilities. Delegation can be used to respond to a particular action or to retrieve data from an external source without needing to know the underlying type of that source.

Listing 12-3 defines two protocols for use with a random number guessing game.

Listing 12-3. Protocol Definitions

```
protocol RandomNumberGame {
    var machine: Machine { get }
    func play()
}
protocol RandomNumberGameDelegate {
    func gameDidStart(game: RandomNumberGame)
    func game(game: RandomNumberGame, didStartNewTurnWithGuess randomGuess: Int)
    func gameDidEnd(game: RandomNumberGame)
}
```

The RandomNumberGame protocol is a protocol that can be adopted by any game that involves random number generating and guessing. The RandomNumberGameDelegate protocol can be adopted by any type of class to track the progress of a RandomNumberGame protocol.

Protocol and Delegation Example

In this section, I will show you how to create a more sophisticated random number guessing app to illustrate how to use protocols and delegation. The app's home view displays the user's guess and whether the guess was high, low, or correct, as shown in Figure 12-3.

Figure 12-3. Guessing Game App home view

When the user taps Guess Random Number, the user is taken to an input screen to enter their guess, as shown in Figure 12-4.

Figure 12-4. Guessing Game App user input view

When the user enters the guess, the delegate method passes back to the home view the guess, and the home view displays the result.

Getting Started

Follow these steps to create the app:

1. Create a new Swift project based on the Single View Application template, name it **RandomNumberDelegates**, and save it, as shown in Figure 12-5.

Figure 12-5. Creating the project

2. Select the `Main.storyboard` file, and from the File Inspector, uncheck **Use Auto Layout** and select **Disable Size Classes**. This will enable you to focus on just one device, the iPhone 5, and not worry about Auto Layout, as shown in Figure 12-6.

Figure 12-6. *Turning off Auto Layout*

3. From the Document Outline, select **View Controller** and **Editor ➤ Embed In ➤ Navigation Controller**. This embeds your scene in a **Navigation Controller** and enables you to easily transition back and forth to new scenes, as shown in Figure 12-7.

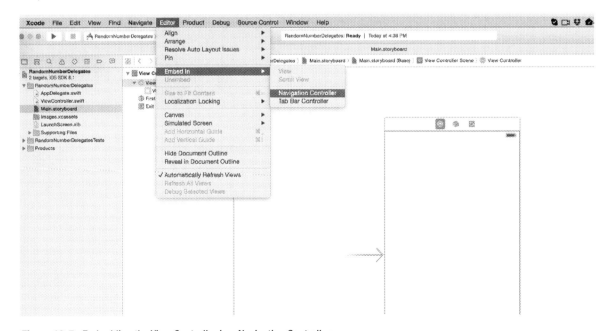

Figure 12-7. *Embedding the View Controller in a Navigation Controller*

4. In the **View Controller**, add two **Label** objects and two **Button** objects along with four **Outlet** objects, which will control the view, as shown in Figure 12-8 and Listing 12-4.

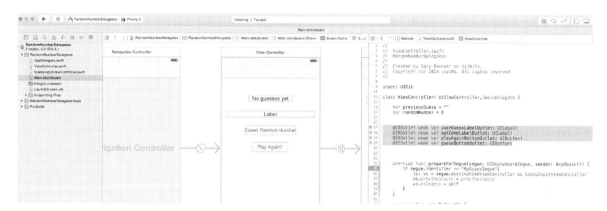

Figure 12-8. *Outlets necessary to control the view*

Listing 12-4. IBAction function

```
47      //event triggered by playAgain Button
48      @IBAction func playAgainAction(sender: AnyObject) {
49          createRandomNumber()
50          playAgainButtonOutlet.hidden = true //only show the button when the user guessed the right #
51          guessButtonOutlet.hidden = false //show the button
52          outComeLabelOutlet.text = ""
53          userGuessLabel.text = "New Game"
54          previousGuess = ""
55      }
```

5. Add the code in Listing 12-5 for the functions to handle when the user guesses a number and to handle creating a random number.

Listing 12-5. User Guess Delegate Function and createRandomNumber Function

```
57  //function called from the GuessInputViewController when the user taps on  the Save Button button
58      func userDidFinish(controller: GuessInputViewController, guess: String) {
59          userGuessLabel.text = "The guess was " +  guess
60          previousGuess = guess
61          var numberGuess = guess.toInt()
62          if (numberGuess > randomNumber){
63                  outComeLabelOutlet.text = "Guess too high"
64          }
65          else if (numberGuess < randomNumber) {
66              outComeLabelOutlet.text = "Guess too low"
67          }
```

```
68          else {
69              outComeLabelOutlet.text = "Guess is correct"
70              playAgainButtonOutlet.hidden = false //show the play again button
71              guessButtonOutlet.hidden = true //hide the guess again number
72          }
73          //pops the GuessInputViewController off the stack
74          controller.navigationController?.popViewControllerAnimated(true)
75      }
76      //creates the random number
77      func createRandomNumber() {
78          randomNumber = Int(arc4random_uniform(100)) //get a random number between 0-100
79          println("The random number is: \(randomNumber)") //lets us cheat
80          return
81      }
```

6. Declare and initialize the two variables on lines 13 and 14 in Listing 12-6.

Listing 12-6. Variable declarations and intializations

```
11 class ViewController: UIViewController,GuessDelegate {
12
13     var previousGuess = ""
14     var randomNumber = 0
15
16
17     @IBOutlet weak var userGuessLabelOutlet: UILabel!
18     @IBOutlet weak var outComeLabelOutlet: UILabel!
19     @IBOutlet weak var playAgainButtonOutlet: UIButton!
20     @IBOutlet weak var guessButtonOutlet: UIButton!!
```

7. Modify the function viewDidLoad() to handle how the view should look when it first appears and create the random number to guess, as shown in Listing 12-7.

Listing 12-7. viewDidLoad function

```
32 override func viewDidLoad() {
33         super.viewDidLoad()
34         // Do any additional setup after loading the view, typically from a nib.
35         self.createRandomNumber()
36         playAgainButtonOutlet.hidden = true;
37         outComeLabelOutlet.text = ""
38
39     }
```

8. Now you need to create a view to enable the user to enter their guess. In the Storyboard.swift file, drag a new **View Controller** next to the home view controller and create a **Label**, **Text Field**, and **Button**. For the **Text Field** object, in the **Placeholder** property, type **Number between 0-100**, as shown in Figure 12-9.

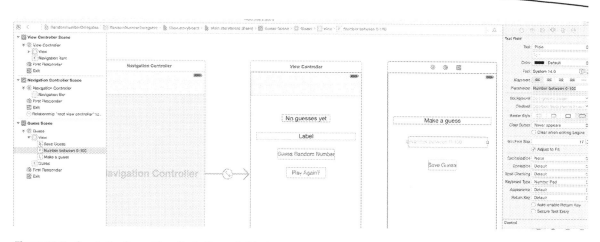

Figure 12-9. *Create the Guess View Controller and objects*

9. You need to create a class for the **Guess Input View Controller**. Create a Swift file and save it as GuessInputViewController.swift. Choose **File ➤ New ➤ File**, choose **iOS ➤ Source ➤ Cocoa Touch Class**, and then name the class **GuessInputViewController**, subclassed from UIViewController, as shown in Figure 12-10.

Figure 12-10. *Create the GuessInputViewController.swift file*

10. Let's associate the GuessInputViewController class with the **Guess View Controller** created in step 8. From the Main.storyboard file, select **Guess Input View Controller ➤ Identity Inspector** and select or type **GuessInputViewController** in the **Class** field, as shown in Figure 12-11.

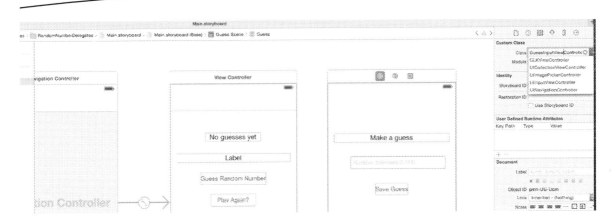

Figure 12-11. *Creating the GuessInputViewController.swift file*

Now let's create and connect the actions and outlets in the GuessInputViewController class, as shown in Listing 12-8.

Listing 12-8. Class listing

```
9   import UIKit
10
11  //protocol used to send data back the home view controller's userDidFinish
12  protocol GuessDelegate{
13      func userDidFinish(controller:GuessInputViewController,guess:String)
14  }
15
16  class GuessInputViewController: UIViewController,  UITextFieldDelegate {
17
18      var delegate:GuessDelegate? = nil
19      var previousGuess:String = ""
20
21
22      @IBOutlet weak var guessLabelOutlet: UILabel!
23      @IBOutlet weak var guessTextOutlet: UITextField!
24
25      override func viewDidLoad() {
26          super.viewDidLoad()
27
28          // Do any additional setup after loading the view.
29          if(!previousGuess.isEmpty){
30              guessLabelOutlet.text = "Your previous guess was \(previousGuess)"
31          }
32          guessTextOutlet.becomeFirstResponder()
33      }
34
35      override func didReceiveMemoryWarning() {
36          super.didReceiveMemoryWarning()
37          // Dispose of any resources that can be recreated.
38      }
39
```

```
40     @IBAction func saveGuessAction(sender: AnyObject) {
41         if (delegate != nil){
42             delegate!.userDidFinish(self, guess: guessTextOutlet.text)
43         }
44     }
45
46 }
```

> **Note**   To see the bound rectangles around your controls in your storyboard, as shown in Figure 12-11, choose **Editor ➤ Canvas ➤ Show Bounds Rectangle**.

11. You are almost done. You need to connect the scene with a segue. A segue enables you to transition from one scene to another. Control-drag from the **Guess Random Number** button to the **Guess Input View Controller** and select **Push** as the Action, as shown in Figure 12-12.

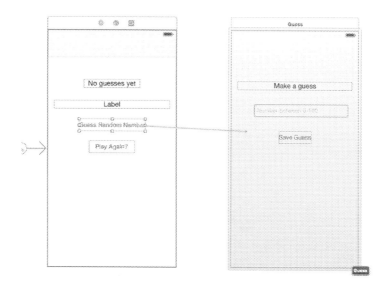

Figure 12-12. Creating the segue that transitions scenes when the Guess Random Number button is tapped

12. Now you need to give the segue an identifier. Click the segue arrow, select the Attributes Inspector, and name the segue **MyGuessSegue**, as shown in Figure 12-13.

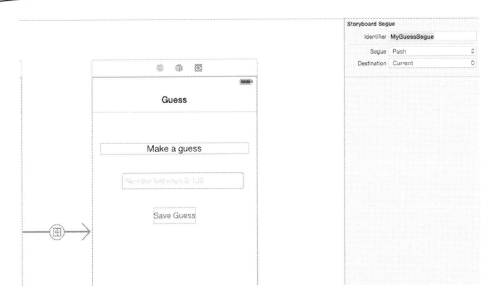

Figure 12-13. Creating the segue identifier

> **Note**   Make sure you press the Return key when you type in the segue identifier. Xcode may not pick up the property change if you don't hit Return.

Now you need to write the code to handle the segue. In the `ViewController` class, add the code in Listing 12-9.

Listing 12-9. prepareForSegue Function

```
24 override func prepareForSegue(segue: UIStoryboardSegue, sender: AnyObject!) {
25       if segue.identifier == "MyGuessSegue"{
26           let vc = segue.destinationViewController as GuessInputViewController
27           vc.previousGuess = previousGuess // passes the last guess the previousGuess property
                                                       in the GuessInputViewController
28           vc.delegate = self
29       }
30   }
```

When the user taps the Guess Random Number button, the segue gets called, and the function `prepareForSegue` gets called. You first check to see whether it was the MyGuessSegue segue. You then populate the vc variable with the `GuessInputViewController`.

Lines 27 and 28 pass the `previousGuess` number and delegate to the `GuessInputViewController`.

13. Finally, if you haven't added the GuessDelegate delegate to the ViewController class, do it now, as shown in Listing 12-10.

Listing 12-10. ViewController Class with GuessDelegate listed

```
11 class ViewController: UIViewController,GuessDelegate {
12
13    var previousGuess = ""
14    var randomNumber = 0
```

How Does It Work

Here is how the code works:

▓ When the user taps Guess Random Number, prepareForSegue is called. See line 25 in Listing 12-9.

▓ Because the ViewController conforms to the GuessDelegate (see line 11 in Listing 12-10), you can pass self to the delegate in GuessInputViewController.

▓ The GuessInputViewController scene is displayed.

▓ When the user guesses a number and taps Save Guess, the saveGuessAction is called (see line 40 in Listing 12-8).

▓ Since you passed ViewController to the delegate, it can call the previousGuess back in the ViewController.swift file (see line 42 in Listing 12-8).

▓ Now you can determine whether the user guessed the correct answer and pop the GuessInputViewController view from the stack (see line 74 in Listing 12-5).

Summary

In this chapter, I covered why multiple inheritance is not used in Swift and how protocols and delegates work. When you think of delegates, think of helper classes. When your class conforms to a protocol, the delegate's functions help your class.

You should be familiar with the following terms:

▓ Multiple inheritance

▓ Protocols

▓ Delegates

Exercise

▓ Change the random number the computer guesses from 0-100 to 0-50.

▓ In the main scene, display how many guesses the user has made trying to guess the random number.

▓ In the main scene, display how many games the user has played.

Chapter 13

Introducing the Xcode Debugger

Not only is Xcode provided free of charge on Apple's developer site and the Mac App Store, but it is a great tool. Aside from being able to use it to create the next great Mac, iPhone, and iPad apps, Xcode has a debugger built right into the tool.

What exactly is a debugger? Well, let's get something straight—programs do *exactly* what they are written to do, but sometimes what is written isn't exactly what the program is really meant to do. This can mean the program crashes or just doesn't do something that is expected. Whatever the case, when a program doesn't work as planned, the program is said to have *bugs*. The process of going through the code and fixing these problems is called *debugging*.

There is still some debate as to the real origin of the term *bug*, but one well-documented case from 1947 involved the late Rear Admiral Grace Hopper, a Naval reservist and programmer at the time. Hopper and her team were trying to solve a problem with the Harvard Mark II computer. One team member found a moth in the circuitry that was causing the problem with one of the relays. Hooper was later quoted as saying, "From then on, when anything went wrong with a computer, we said it had bugs in it."[1]

Regardless of the origin, the term stuck, and programmers all over the world use debuggers, such as the one built into Xcode, to help find bugs in programs. But people are the real debuggers; debugging tools merely help programmers locate problems. No debugger, whatever the name might imply, fixes problems all on its own.

This chapter will highlight some of the more important features of the Xcode debugger and will explain how to use them. Once you are finished with this chapter, you should have a good enough understanding of the Xcode debugger and of the debugging process in general to allow you to search for and fix the majority of programming issues.

---

[1]Michael Moritz, Alexander L. Taylor III, and Peter Stoler, "The Wizard Inside the Machine," *Time,* Vol.123, no. 16: pp. 56–63

Getting Started with Debugging

If you've ever watched a movie in slow motion just so you can catch a detail you can't see when the movie is played at full speed, you've used a tool to do something a little like debugging. The idea that playing the movie frame by frame will reveal the detail you are looking for is the same sort of idea you apply when debugging a program. With a program, sometimes it becomes necessary to slow things down a bit to see what's happening. The debugger allows you to do this using two main features: setting a breakpoint and stepping through the program line by line—more on these two features in a bit. Let's first look at how to get to the debugger and what it looks like.

First you need to load an application. The examples in this chapter use the Bookstore project from Chapter 8, so open Xcode and load the Bookstore project.

Second, make sure the Debug configuration is chosen on the Run scheme, as shown in Figure 13-1. To edit the current scheme, choose Product ➤ Scheme ➤ Edit Scheme from the main menu. Debug is the default selection, so you probably won't have to change this. This step is important because if the configuration is set to Release, debugging will not work at all.

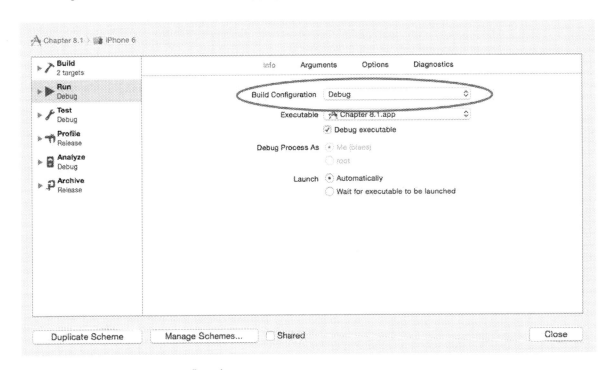

Figure 13-1. *Selecting the Debug configuration*

While this book won't discuss Xcode schemes, just know that by default Xcode provides both a Release configuration and a Debug configuration for any Mac OS X or iOS project you create. The main difference as it pertains to this chapter is that a Release configuration doesn't add any program information that is necessary for debugging an application, whereas the Debug configuration does.

Setting Breakpoints

To see what's going on in a program, you need to make the program pause at certain points that you as a programmer are interested in. A *breakpoint* allows you to do this. In Figure 13-2, there is a breakpoint on line 25 of the program. To set this, simply place the cursor over the line number (not the program text, but the number 25 to the left of the program text) and click once. You will see a small blue arrow behind the line number. This lets you know that a breakpoint is set.

Figure 13-2. Your first breakpoint

If line numbers are not being displayed, simply choose Xcode ➤ Preferences from the main menu, click the Text Editing tab, and select the "Line numbers" check box.

You can also remove the breakpoint by dragging the breakpoint to the left or right of the line number column and then dropping it. In Figure 13-3, the breakpoint has been dragged to the left of the column. During the drag-and-drop process, the breakpoint will turn into a puff of smoke. You can also right-click (or Control-click) the breakpoint, and you will be given the option to delete or disable a breakpoint. Disabling a breakpoint is convenient if you think you might need it again in the future.

```
21      super.viewDidLoad()
22      // Do any additional setup after loading the view, typically from a nib.
23      self.navigationItem.leftBarButtonItem = self.editButtonItem()
24
25      let addButton = UIBarButtonItem(barButtonSystemItem: .Add, target: self, action: "insertNewObject:")
        ...                         ...BarButtonItem = addButton
Edit Breakpoint...
Disable Breakpoint              /Warning() {
                                  ing()
Delete Breakpoint               es that can be recreated.

Reveal in Breakpoint Navigator
                                AnyObject) {
35      objects.insertObject(NSDate(), atIndex: 0)
36      let indexPath = NSIndexPath(forRow: 0, inSection: 0)
37      self.tableView.insertRowsAtIndexPaths([indexPath], withRowAnimation: .Automatic)
38    }
```

Figure 13-3. Right-clicking a breakpoint

Setting and deleting breakpoints are pretty straightforward tasks.

Using the Breakpoint Navigator

With small projects, knowing where all the breakpoints are isn't necessarily hard. However, once a project gets larger than, say, your small MyBookstore application, managing all the breakpoints could be a little more difficult. Fortunately, Xcode 6.1 provides a simple method to list all the breakpoints in an application; it's called the Breakpoint navigator. Just click the Breakpoint Navigator icon in the navigation selector bar, as shown in Figure 13-4.

Figure 13-4. Accessing the Breakpoint navigator in Xcode 6.1

Once you've clicked the icon, the navigator will list all the breakpoints currently defined in the application. From here, clicking a breakpoint will take you to the source file with the breakpoint. You can also easily delete and disable breakpoints from here.

To disable/enable a breakpoint in the Breakpoint navigator, click the blue breakpoint icon in the list (or wherever it appears). Don't click the line; it has to be the little blue icon, as shown in Figure 13-5.

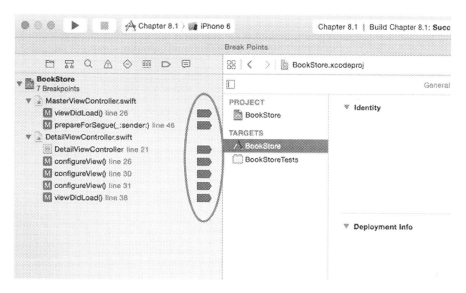

Figure 13-5. *Using the Breakpoint navigator to enable/disable a breakpoint*

It is sometimes handy to disable a breakpoint instead of deleting it, especially if you plan to put the breakpoint back in the same place again. The debugger will not stop on these faded breakpoints, but they remain in place so they can be conveniently enabled and act as a marker to an important area in the code.

It's also possible to delete breakpoints from the Breakpoint navigator. Simply select one or more breakpoints and press the Delete key. Make sure you select the correct breakpoints to delete since there is no undo feature.

It's also possible to select the file associated with the breakpoints. In this case, if you delete the file listed in the Breakpoint navigator and press Delete, all breakpoints in that file will be deleted.

Please note that breakpoints are categorized by the file that they appear in. In Figure 13-5, the files are DetailViewController.m and MasterViewController.m, with the breakpoints listed below those file names. Figure 13-6 shows an example of what a file looks like with more than a single breakpoint.

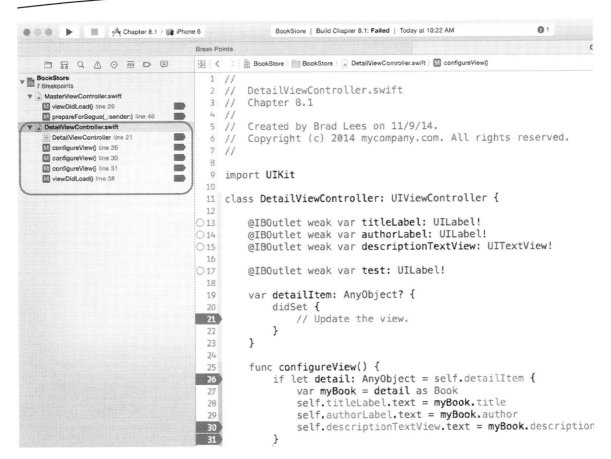

Figure 13-6. A file with several breakpoints

Debugging Basics

Set a breakpoint on the statement shown in Figure 13-2. Next, as shown in Figure 13-7, click the Run button to compile the project and start running it within the Xcode debugger.

Figure 13-7. The Build and Debug buttons in the Xcode toolbar

Once the project builds, the debugger will start. The screen will show the debugging windows, and the program will stop execution on the line statement, as shown in Figure 13-8.

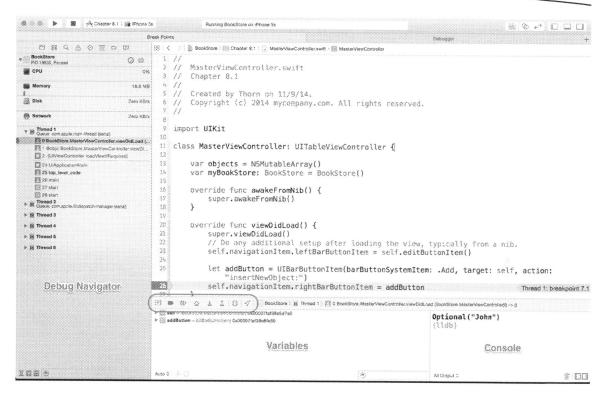

Figure 13-8. The Debugger view with execution stopped on line 25

The Debugger view adds some additional windows. The following are the different parts of the Debugger view shown in Figure 13-8:

1. *Debugger controls (circled in Figure 13-8)*: The debugging controls can pause, continue, step over, step into, and step out of statements in the program. The stepping controls are used most often. The first button on the left is used to show or hide the debugger view. In Figure 13-8, the debugger view is shown.

2. *Variables*: The Variables view displays the variables currently in scope. Clicking the little triangle just to the left of a variable name will expand it.

3. *Console*: The output window will show useful information in the event of a crash or exception. Also, any NSLog of `println` output goes here.

4. *Debug navigator*: The stack trace shows the call stack as well as all the threads currently active in the program. The stack is a hierarchical view of what methods are being called. For example, `main` calls `UIApplication`, and `UIApplication` calls the `UIViewController` class. These method calls "stack" up until they finally return.

Working with the Debugger Controls

As mentioned previously, once the debugger starts, the view changes. What appears are the debugging controls (circled in Figure 13-8). The controls are fairly straightforward and are explained in Table 13-1.

Table 13-1. Xcode Debugging Controls

Control	Description
▶ ■	Clicking the Stop button will stop the execution of the program. If the iPhone or iPad emulator is running the application, it will also stop as if the user clicked the Home button on the device. Clicking the Run button starts debugging. If the application is currently in debug mode, clicking the Run button again will restart debugging the application from the beginning; it's like stopping and then starting again.
❙▷	Clicking this causes the program to pause or continue execution. The program will continue running until it ends, the Stop button is clicked, or the program runs into another breakpoint.
⌃	When the debugger stops on a breakpoint, clicking the Step Over button will cause the debugger to execute the current line of code and stop at the next line of code.
↓	Clicking the Step Into button will cause the debugger to go into the specified function or method. This is important if there is a need to follow code into specific methods or functions. Only methods for which the project has source code can be stepped into.
↑	The Step Out button will cause the current method to finish executing, and the debugger will go back to the caller.

Using the Step Controls

To practice using the step controls, let's step into a method. As the name implies, the Step Into button follows program execution into the method or function that is highlighted. Select the DetailViewController.swift file on the left side. Then set a breakpoint on line 38, which is the call to self.configureView(). Click the Run button and select a book from the list. Your screen should look similar to Figure 13-9.

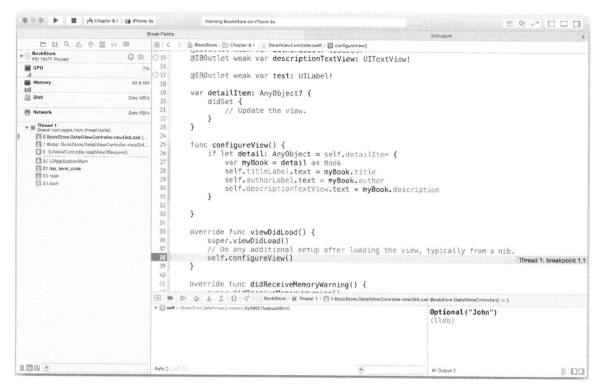

Figure 13-9. *The debugger stopped on line 38*

Click the Step Into button, 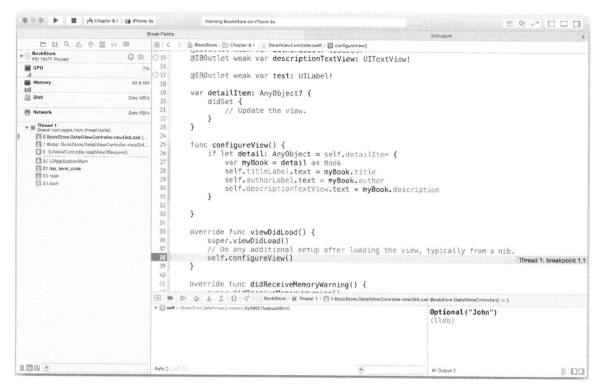 which will cause the debugger to go into the configureView() method of the Bookstore object. The screen should look like Figure 13-10.

Figure 13-10. *Stepping into the* init *method of the Bookstore object*

The control Step Over, , continues execution of the program but doesn't go into a method. It simply executes the method and continues to the next line. Step Out, , is a little like the opposite of Step Into. If the Step Out button is clicked, the current method continues execution until it finishes. The debugger then returns to the line before Step Into was clicked. For example, if the Step Into button is clicked on the line shown in Figure 13-9 and then the Step Out button is clicked, the debugger will return to the viewDidLoad() method of the DetailViewController.swift file on the statement shown in Figure 13-9 (line 38 in the example), which was the line where Step Into was clicked.

Looking at the Thread Window and Call Stack

As mentioned earlier, the Debug navigator displays the current thread. However, it also displays the call stack. If you look at the difference between Figures 13-9 and 13-10 as far as the thread window goes, you can see that Figure 13-10 has the configureView method listed because DetailViewController calls the configureView method.

Now, the call stack is not simply a list of functions that *have* been called; rather, it's a list of functions that are currently *being* called. That's an important distinction. Once the configureView method is finished and returns (line 33), configureView will no longer appear in the call stack. You can think of a call stack almost like a breadcrumb trail. The trail shows you how to get back to where you started.

Debugging Variables

It is possible to view some information about a variable (other than its memory address) by hovering over the variable in the code. When you get to where the value of a variable has been assigned in the local scope, you will see the variable in the bottom Variables view. In Figure 13-11, you can see the newBook variable, and it has a title of Swift for Absolute Beginners. You can also see that there is no author or description assigned. In debugging, when you are stopped on a line, it is before the line is executed. This means that even though you are paused on the line to assign the author property, it has not been assigned yet.

Figure 13-11. *Viewing a variable value*

Position the cursor over any place the newBook variable appears and click the disclosure triangle to display the Book object. You should see what is displayed in Figure 13-12.

Figure 13-12. Hovering over the newBook variable reveals some information

Hovering over the newBook variable reveals its information. In Figure 13-12, you can see the newBook variable expanded.

Dealing with Code Errors and Warnings

While coding errors and warnings aren't really part of the Xcode 6 debugger, fixing them is part of the entire debugging process. Before a program can be run (with or without the debugger), all errors must be fixed. Warnings won't stop a program from building, but they could cause issues during program execution. It's best not to have warnings at all.

Errors

Let's take a look at a couple of types of errors. To start, let's add an error to the code. On line 14 of the MasterViewController.swift file, change the following:

```
var myBookStore: BookStore = BookStore()
```

to the following:

```
var myBookStore: BookStore = BookStore[]
```

Save the changes and then build the project by pressing ⌘+B. There will be an error, as shown in Figure 13-13, that may show up immediately or after the build.

Figure 13-13. Viewing the error in Xcode

Next, move over to the Issue navigator window, as shown in Figure 13-14, by clicking the triangle with the exclamation point. This view shows all the errors and warnings currently in the program—not just the current file, `MainViewController.swift`, but all the files. Errors are displayed as a white exclamation point inside a red octagon. In this case, you have one error. If the error doesn't fit on the screen or is hard to read, simply hover over the error on the Issue navigator, and the full error will be displayed.

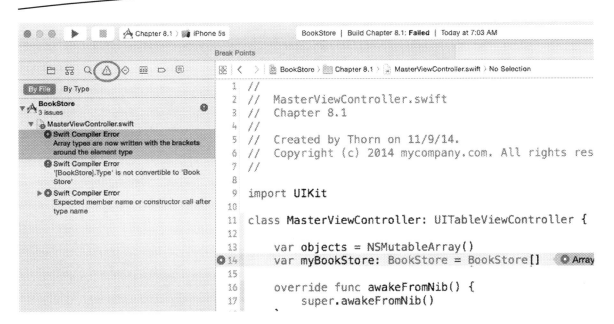

Figure 13-14. Viewing the Issue navigator

Generally, the error points to the problem. In the previous case, the BookStore object was initialized as an array rather than an object.

Go ahead and fix the error by changing [ ] to ( ).

Warnings

Warnings indicate potential problems with the program. As mentioned, warnings won't stop a program from building but may cause issues during program execution. It's outside the scope of this book to cover those warnings that may or may not cause problems during program execution; however, it's good practice to eliminate all warnings from a program.

Add the following code to the MasterViewController.swift viewDidLoad method:

```
if (false){
    println("False")
}
```

The println command will never be executed because false will never be equal to true. Build the project by pressing ⌘+B. A warning will be displayed as shown in Figure 13-15.

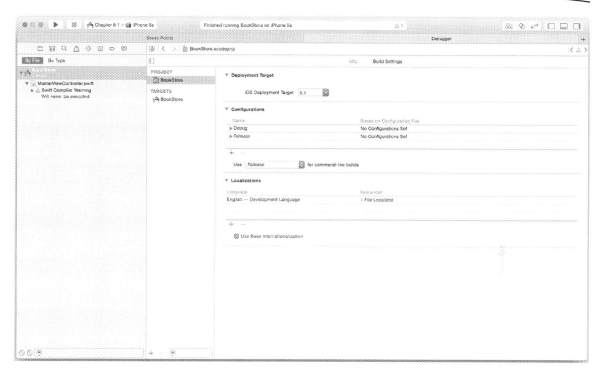

Figure 13-15. *Viewing the warnings in the Issue navigator*

Clicking the first warning in the Issue navigator will show you the code that is causing the first problem, as shown in Figure 13-16.

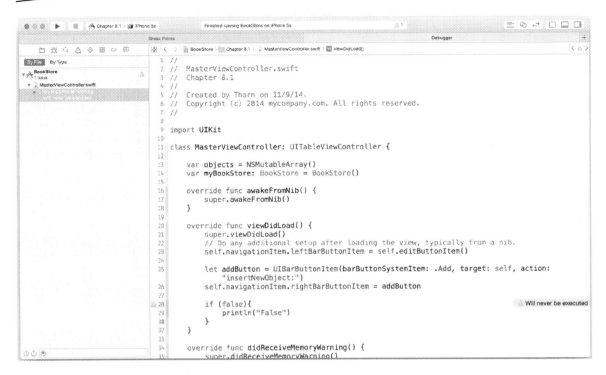

Figure 13-16. Viewing your first warning

In the main window, you can see the warning. In fact, this warning gives you a clue as to the problem with the code. The warning states the following:

"Will never be executed"

This is a simple example of a warning. You can receive warnings for many things such as unused variables, incomplete delegate implementations, and unexecutable code. It is good practice to clean up the warnings in your code to avoid issues down the road.

Summary

This chapter covered the high-level features of the free Apple Xcode debugger. Regardless of price, Xcode is an excellent debugger. Specifically, in this chapter, you learned the following:

- The origins of the term *bug* and what a debugger is
- The high-level features of the Xcode debugger
  - Breakpoints
  - Stepping through a program

- How to use the debugging controls
  - Continue
  - Step Over
  - Step Into
  - Step Out
- Working with the various debugger views
  - Threads (call stack)
  - Variables
  - Text editor
  - Output
- Looking at program variables
- Dealing with errors and warnings

14

A Swift iPhone App

In Chapter 8 you created a basic bookstore iPhone app with Swift. In this chapter, you will add some features to the app to make it a bit more functional and use many of the technologies you have learned in this book, such as creating a class, using delegates and protocols, and using actions and outlets. You'll also learn about some new techniques such as switches, `UIAlertView`, and landmarks.

Let's Get Started

The bookstore example in Chapter 8 enabled you to view books in your bookstore in a Table View and then tap the book to see its details. In this chapter you will add the following capabilities to the Chapter 8 bookstore app:

- Adding a book
- Deleting a book
- Modifying a book

See Figures 14-1 and 14-2.

Figure 14-1. Add book functionality

Figure 14-2. *Adding edit and delete functionality along with using a UISwitch*

Using the app you created in Chapter 8, add a Button Bar Item by dragging the Button Bar Item object to the Right Button Bar location in the Main.storyboard file. Change the Button Bar Item Identifier to Add. This will give you the plus sign (+) icon, as shown in Figure 14-3.

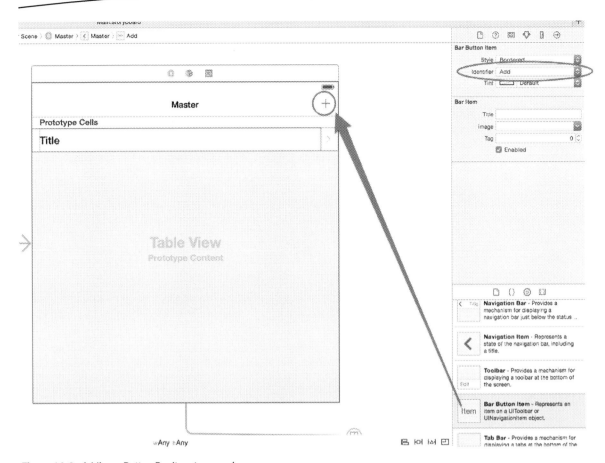

Figure 14-3. Adding a Button Bar Item to your view

Modify and add the code that will handle a showDetail method and a addBookSegue segue in the MasterViewController.swift file, starting at line 46 in Listing 14-1. The code will transition to the scene that will add a book to the list and pass the view to a delegate. The next step will be to define the AddBookViewController.

Listing 14-1. The prepareForSegue function

```
40  // MARK:  Segues
41
42 override func prepareForSegue(segue: UIStoryboardSegue, sender: AnyObject?) {
43        if segue.identifier == "showDetail" {
44            if let indexPath = self.tableView.indexPathForSelectedRow() {
45                let selectedBook:Book = myBookStore.theBookStore[indexPath.row]
46                let vc = segue.destinationViewController as DetailViewController
47                vc.detailItem = selectedBook
48                vc.delegate = self
49            }
50        }
```

```
51          else if segue.identifier == "addBookSegue" {
52              let vc = segue.destinationViewController as AddBookViewController
53              vc.delegate = self
54          }
55      }
```

> **Note**   Something new in Swift is on line 40: "// MARK: - Segues". // MARK: is called a *landmark*.
> It is replacement of the pragma mark, which is used in Objective-C. Landmarks help break up the code in
> the jump bar and enable you to quickly get to sections of code indicated by the landmark. When you type
> something following // MARK:, Xcode places the landmark in the jump bar's drop-down, as shown in
> Figure 14-4. If you just type **// MARK: -** , Xcode adds a line separator in the jump bar drop-down. Swift also
> supports // TODO: and // FIXME: landmarks to annotate your code and lists them in the jump bar.

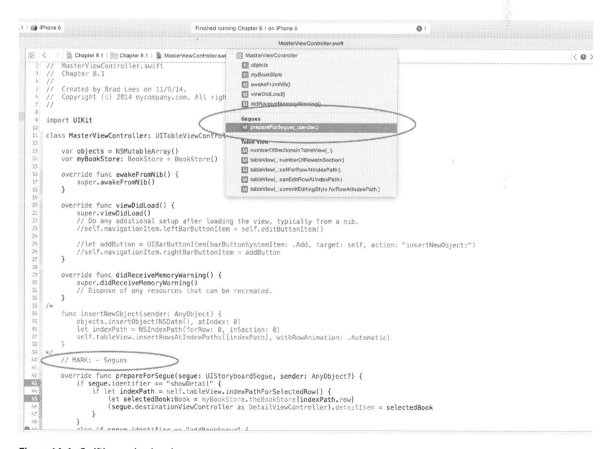

Figure 14-4. Swift's new landmarks

Now add the new view controller `AddBookViewController` mentioned in line 52 in Listing 14-1. Add a View Controller object to the storyboard by dragging a View Controller to the `Main.storyboard` file. Then add the objects in Figure 14-5 to enable the user to add a new book. Feel free to move the scenes around to make it clear how they relate to each other, as shown in Figure 14-5.

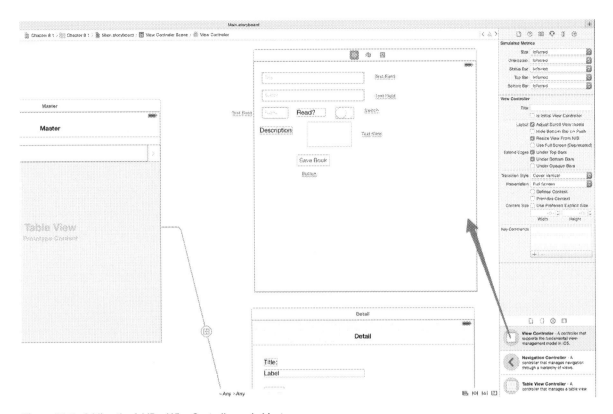

Figure 14-5. Adding the AddBookViewController and objects

Add a Show Segue object from the Add Button Bar Item to the new View Controller by Control-dragging dragging or right-clicking and dragging from the Add Button Bar Item to the new View Controller, as shown Figure 14-6.

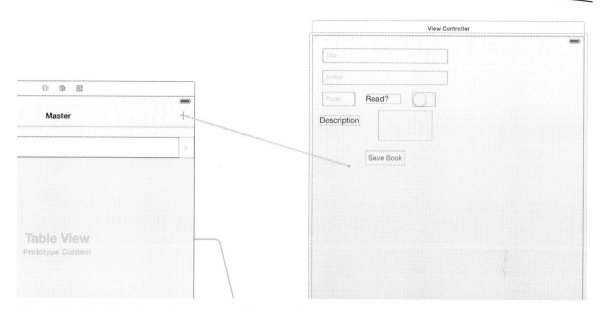

Figure 14-6. *Add a Show Segue object to the new View Controller*

Label the Segue object by clicking the segue arrow and labeling the Identifier as **addBookSegue**, as shown in Figure 14-7.

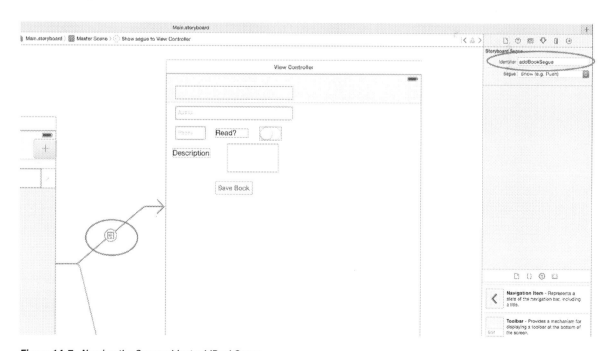

Figure 14-7. *Naming the Segue object addBookSegue*

Now you need to create a Swift class to go with the new View Controller. Create a new file and Cocoa class and name it **AddBookViewController**, as shown in Figure 14-8. Make sure you select a subclass of UIViewController.

Figure 14-8. Adding the AddBookViewController class

Now you have to associate the new AddBookViewController class to the new View Controller. Select the View Controller, and in the Identity Inspector, type **AddBookViewController** for the class, as shown in Figure 14-9.

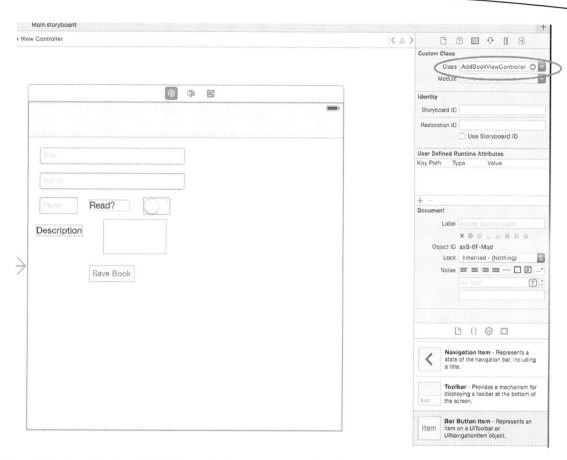

Figure 14-9. *Associating the AddBookViewController class to the new View Controller*

Add the code to the AddBookViewController class. Open the AddBookViewController.swift file and add the code shown in Listing 14-2.

Listing 14-2. The AddBookViewController.swift file

```
 9 import UIKit
10
11 protocol BookStoreDelegate {
12     func newBook(controller: AnyObject, newBook: Book)
13     func editBook(controller: AnyObject, editBook: Book)
14     func deleteBook(controller: AnyObject)
15 }
16
17
18 class AddBookViewController: UIViewController {
19     var book = Book()
20     var delegate: BookStoreDelegate? = nil
21     var read = false
22     var editBook = false
23
```

```
24      @IBOutlet weak var titleText: UITextField!
25      @IBOutlet weak var authorText: UITextField!
26      @IBOutlet weak var pagesText: UITextField!
27      @IBOutlet weak var descriptionText: UITextView!
28
29      @IBOutlet weak var switchOutlet: UISwitch!
30
31
32      override func viewDidLoad() {
33          super.viewDidLoad()
34          if(editBook == true){
35              self.title = "Edit Book"
36              titleText.text = book.title
37              authorText.text = book.author
38              pagesText.text = String(book.pages)
39              descriptionText.text = book.description
40              if (book.readThisBook){
41                  switchOutlet.on = true
42              }
43              else {
44                  switchOutlet.on = false
45              }
46          }
47
48      }
49
50      override func didReceiveMemoryWarning() {
51          super.didReceiveMemoryWarning()
52          // Dispose of any resources that can be recreated.
53      }
54
55
56      @IBAction func saveBookAction(sender: UIButton) {
57          book.title = titleText.text
58          book.author = authorText.text
59          book.description = descriptionText.text
60          book.pages = pagesText.text.toInt()!
61          if(switchOutlet.on) {
62            book.readThisBook = true
63          }
64          else {
65            book.readThisBook = false
66          }
67          if (editBook) {
68              delegate!.editBook(self, editBook:book)
69          }
70          else {
71              delegate!.newBook(self, newBook:book)
72          }
73      }
74 }
```

To the Book class, add two properties: pages and readThisBook, as shown in lines 15 and 16 in Listing 14-3.

Listing 14-3. Book Class changes

```
11 class Book {
12     var title: String = ""
13     var author: String = ""
14     var description: String = ""
15     var pages: Int = 0
16     var readThisBook: Bool = false
17 }
```

Switches

Connect the outlets in the AddBookViewController class by dragging them from their open circles to the controls, as shown in Figure 14-10.

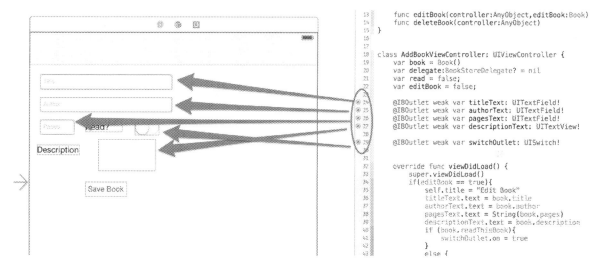

Figure 14-10. Connecting the outlets

Connect the saveBookAction action by dragging the outlet circle to the Save Book button, as shown in Figure 14-11.

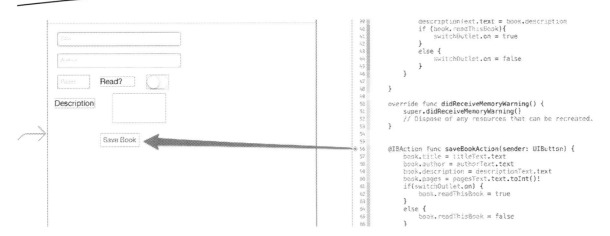

Figure 14-11. *Connecting the saveBookAction*

In the DetailViewController class, add the code shown in Listing 14-4.

Listing 14-4. New Properties

```
20    @IBOutlet weak var pagesOutlet: UILabel!
21    @IBOutlet weak var switchOutlet: UISwitch!
22
23    var delegate: BookStoreDelegate? = nil
24
25    var myBook = Book()
```

Alert Views

You want the DetailViewController to conform to the UIAlertViewDelegate. This will enable the DetailViewController to respond to delegate messages when the user taps the Yes button in an alertView acknowledging that the user is deleting a book.

In the DetailViewController.swift file, add the UIAlertViewDelegate, as shown in Listing 14-5.

Listing 14-5. Adding the UIAlertViewDelegate

```
class DetailViewController: UIViewController, UIAlertViewDelegate {
```

Add the controls for Pages, Read, and Edit for the DetailViewController. Connect the outlets by dragging the open circles to their controls, as shown in Figure 14-12.

Figure 14-12. Adding the Pages and Read outlets

The Read switch is disabled in this view by unchecking the "enabled" property in the Attributes Inspector.

Add the code for displaying an AlertView when the Delete Button Bar is tapped, as shown in Listing 14-6.

Listing 14-6. Displaying an UIAlertView

```
52    @IBAction func deleteBookAction(sender: UIBarButtonItem) {
53        let alert = UIAlertView()
54        alert.title = "Warning"
55        alert.message = "Delete this book?"
56        alert.addButtonWithTitle("No")
57        alert.addButtonWithTitle("Yes")
58        alert.delegate = self
59        alert.show()
60    }
```

Add the alertView delegate function that is called on when the user taps one of the Alert View buttons. See Listing 14-7.

Listing 14-7. Adding an alertView function

```
66 func alertView(View: UIAlertView!, clickedButtonAtIndex buttonIndex: Int){
67
68        switch buttonIndex{
69
70        case 0:
71            println("No")
72        case 1:
73            println("Yes")
74            delegate!.deleteBook(self)
```

```
75        default:
76            println("Default")
77        }
78    }
```

Add the Delete Button Bar Item to the right navigation location and connect it to the action, as shown in Figure 14-13.

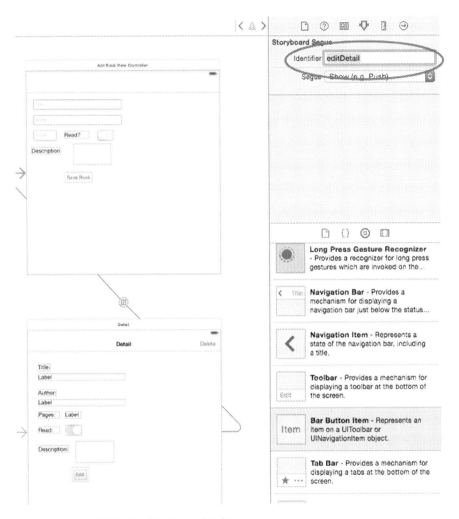

Figure 14-13. Adding the Delete Right Button Bar Item and action

The UIAlertView will warn the user the book currently displayed in the DetailViewController is about to be deleted and will enable the user to decide whether to delete it. The UIAlertView will have two buttons: Yes and No. When the user taps the Delete right Button Bar Item, the UIAlertView will be as shown in Figure 14-14 when you are done.

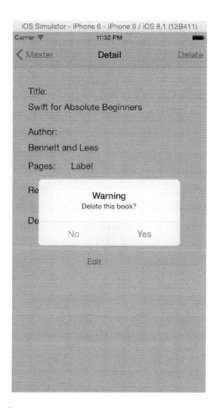

Figure 14-14. UIAlertView being displayed

When the user taps Yes to delete the book, you want to call a deleteBook delegate method as described in the MasterViewController class. You add the delegate property that will store the MasterViewController view in Listing 14-8.

Listing 14-8. Adding the BookStoreDelegate

```
11 class MasterViewController: UITableViewController, BookStoreDelegate {
```

Let's now talk about the three delegate methods: newBook, deleteBook, and editBook, as defined in the AddBookViewController class in Listing 14-2 in lines 11 to 15. Add these three functions at the end MasterViewController class, as shown in Listing 14-9.

Listing 14-9. Conforming to the protocol

```
91 // MARK: - Delegate Methods conforming to the BookStoreDelegate as defined in the
   AddBookViewController
92     func newBook(controller: AnyObject, newBook: Book) {
93         myBookStore.theBookStore.append(newBook)
94         self.tableView.reloadData()
95         let myController = controller as AddBookViewController
96         myController.navigationController?.popToRootViewControllerAnimated(true)
97     }
98
```

```
99     func deleteBook(controller: AnyObject){
100        let indexPath = self.tableView.indexPathForSelectedRow()
101        var row = indexPath?.row
102        myBookStore.theBookStore.removeAtIndex(row!)
103        self.tableView.reloadData()
104        let myController = controller as DetailViewController
105        myController.navigationController?.popToRootViewControllerAnimated(true)
106    }
107
108    func editBook(controller: AnyObject, editBook: Book){
109        let indexPath = self.tableView.indexPathForSelectedRow()
110        var row = indexPath?.row
111        myBookStore.theBookStore.insert(editBook, atIndex: row!)
112        myBookStore.theBookStore.removeAtIndex(row!+1)
113        self.tableView.reloadData()
114        let myController = controller as AddBookViewController
115        myController.navigationController?.popToRootViewControllerAnimated(true)
116    }
```

The function newBook adds a new book to the bookstore; appending the array with the newBook does this, as shown in line 93. Line 94 then reloads the Table View by calling all the Table View delegate methods:

```
numberOfSectionsInTableView
numberOfRowsInSection
cellForRowAtIndexPath
```

Finally, you pop the DetailViewController from the navigation stack by calling popToRootViewControllerAnimated(true). Popping the view from the navigation stack means the view is removed similarly to tapping the Back button.

The function deleteBook removes the book from the bookStore array. First you determine which row was selected in the tableView and use that index to delete the book in the array by calling removeAtIndex(row!), as shown on line 102.

The function editBook enables the user to edit an existing book in the bookStore array. To do this, the function inserts the edited book in the array at the row that was selected, as shown on line 111. Then the function deletes the original book that was pushed down one index when you inserted the book in the array, as shown on line 112.

Now add the Edit button to the bottom of the DetailViewController and add a Show Segue object from the edit button to the AddBookViewController, as shown in Figure 14-15.

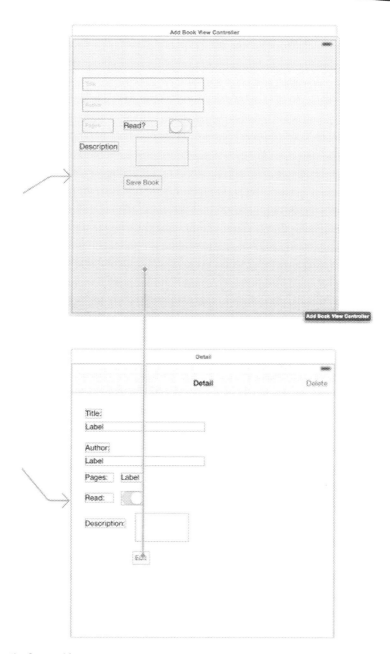

Figure 14-15. Adding the Segue object

Select the Segue object you just created, select the Attributes Inspector, and name the Identifier
editDetail. See Figure 14-16.

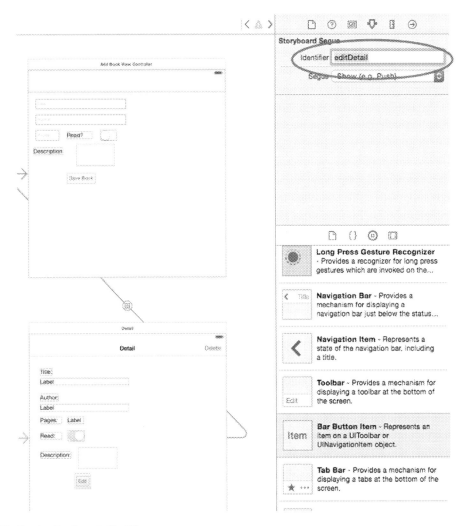

Figure 14-16. Naming the Segue's identifier

Add the prepareForSegue function shown in Listing 14-10 to the bottom of the DetailViewController.swift file.

Listing 14-10. Add the prepareForSegue

```
81 override func prepareForSegue(segue: UIStoryboardSegue, sender: AnyObject?) {
82      if segue.identifier == "editDetail" {
83          let vc = segue.destinationViewController as AddBookViewController
84          vc.delegate = delegate
85          vc.editBook = true
86          vc.book = myBook
87      }
88  }
```

Finally, modify the `configureView` function in the `DetailViewController` to properly populate the pages outlet and switch outlet, as shown in Figure 14-10.

```
29  func configureView() {
30     if let detail: AnyObject = self.detailItem {
31         myBook = detail as Book
32         titleLabel.text = myBook.title
33         authorLabel.text = myBook.author
34         descriptionTextView.text = myBook.description
35         pagesOutlet.text = String(myBook.pages)
36         if(myBook.readThisBook){
37             switchOutlet.on = true
38         }
39         else {
40             switchOutlet.on = false
41         }
42     }
43  }
```

App Summary

Compile and run the app. You should set breakpoints at the delegate functions to watch the program flow. It is a great app to see how delegates can be used to pass information from one view to another.

Additionally, you can add functionality to the app to make the information persistent by using Core Data or `NSUserDefaults`.

What's Next?

You did it! You should have a great foundation to write outstanding apps. The best place to start is with your own idea for an app. Start writing it today. You are going to have lots of questions. That is how you are going to continue to learn. Keep moving forward and don't stop, no matter if you get discouraged sometimes.

If you do get discouraged, visit `www.xcelMe.com/forum`. There are great resources for finding answers to your questions. There is a topic for this book and each chapter in the book. Feel free to post your own questions. The authors of this book help answer the posts. Also, there are free videos on `www.xcelMe.com`. In the live sessions, you can ask questions to Gary Bennett. Just click the Free Videos tab at the top of the page, as shown in Figure 14-17.

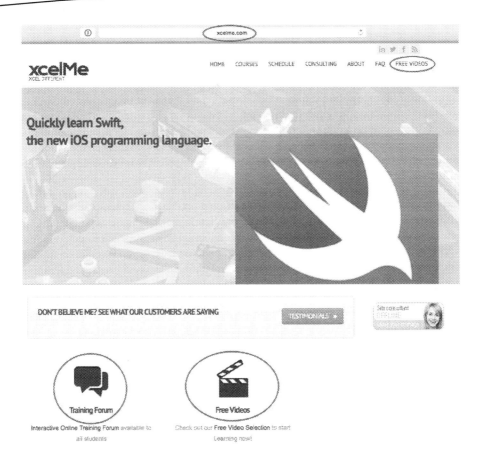

Figure 14-17. Free live Swift training videos

Good luck and have fun!

Exercises

- Add more books to the bookstore using the original program as a guide.

- Enhance the Book class so it can store another attribute—a price or ISBN, for example.

- Add persistence to the app by using Core Data or NSUserDefaults.

Index

Get the eBook for only $10!

Now you can take the weightless companion with you anywhere, anytime. Your purchase of this book entitles you to 3 electronic versions for only $10.

This Apress title will prove so indispensible that you'll want to carry it with you everywhere, which is why we are offering the eBook in 3 formats for only $10 if you have already purchased the print book.

Convenient and fully searchable, the PDF version enables you to easily find and copy code—or perform examples by quickly toggling between instructions and applications. The MOBI format is ideal for your Kindle, while the ePUB can be utilized on a variety of mobile devices.

Go to www.apress.com/promo/tendollars to purchase your companion eBook.